Kevin
Keegan

Michael Hodges is staff writer for *Goal* magazine. He was the last journalist to interview Keegan before his resignation as manager of Newcastle United.

Kevin Keegan

Reluctant Messiah

Michael Hodges

B⬤XTREE

First published in 1997 by Boxtree, an imprint of
Macmillan Publishers Ltd, 25 Eccleston Place, London, SW1W 9NF
and Basingstoke

Associated companies throughout the world

ISBN 0 7522 2476 X

9 8 7 6 5 4 3 2 1

A CIP catalogue record for this book is available
from the British Library

Typeset by SX Composing DTP, Rayleigh, Essex
Printed by Mackays of Chatham plc, Chatham, Kent

Picture Credits
All photographs: Action Images, except 'Swan Song at St James': PA
News

Introduction

Bristol City never had a chance.

The crowd outside St James' Park on Saturday February 8,1992, were in a state of euphoria football supporters don't exhibit unless they have won a trophy. As Newcastle United hadn't contrived to do that since they won the European Fairs Cup in 1969 this was going to have to do and it was something very special. Kevin Keegan, the man who as a player had saved the perpetually tottering club in the early eighties had just returned to the club as manager. And no one, no one at all, thought for a moment that Bristol City, their opponents that day, were going to have any say in the day's celebration. If anything, it was nice of City to turn up. By the end of the afternoon City had been beaten 3-0, Keegan cheered around the park by a population that seemed to have taken leave of its senses and the team, nearly bottom of the old Division Two, were talking about themselves as champions.

Nearly five years later Kevin Keegan walked out of St James'

Park. He left behind a club that was a consistent challenger for the Premiership, had one of the best grounds in Britain and was well established in European competition. But Keegan, who had arrived as a buoyant and happily inexperienced football manager, left a grey and strained figure. Those he left behind were genuinely devastated; Les Ferdinand showed his shock openly on television while Philippe Albert struggled for words. Those that had known him couldn't imagine Newcastle without him. His faithful side-kick Terry McDermott, who had said 'I've got so much respect for the manager, if he asked me to go to Timbuctoo I'd try and find it for him', was left blank-faced and in charge. Tyneside was left confused and uncomprehending. Keegan had lead the club from oblivion to the edge of glory, but more than anything he had been their manager, he had ridden the wave of their enthusiasm; now it seemed it had broken him.

"I do not owe Liverpool anything"

It was a slightly embarrassing appearance at Buckingham Palace. The hired Burton's top hat balanced on the German helmet of agonised curls. Behind him his wife stood, a study in desperately provincial smartness, wearing a pill-box hat, clutch bag gripped to her breast. Either side of him stood Jim Jardine, the former chairman of the Police Federation, and society hairdresser Peter 'Teasy Weasy' Raymond.

Kevin Keegan stepped out to accept the OBE from the Queen. The woman who had been to more FA Cup Finals than any other woman in the world leaned forward to bestow the award widely sought after by light entertainers, serial organisers of charity jumble sales and football players.

Engaging the England star in the polite, loosely informed chit-chat she has made her speciality, the Queen become one of the first people outside of Keegan's family to hear what was to become the *cri de coeur* of his pin-ball journey through the years ahead.

Enquiring how he was feeling about football she was probably not shocked or even bothered when he replied that he felt he had been in the game 'possibly too long'. The Queen may have taken the news equanimously, but it would have provoked a couple of hundred pubs full of spluttered pints in Newcastle-Upon-Tyne.

It was November 9, 1982, and Kevin Keegan was 31. In professional terms it was an age that for a skilled player should mark the beginning of an autumn of mellow fruitfulness on the pitch, an age when guile naturally takes over the duties previously shouldered by physical effort. But Keegan was better than that. Whilst he had the guile he also still had his pace, physical presence and ability to run that had earned him the unfortunate nickname the 'Mighty Mouse'. This is why Arthur Cox, the Newcastle United manager, had signed Keegan that August for £100,000 from Southampton. The whole of Newcastle was transfixed by the proposition of the city's football club finally winning something, even if it was the modest target of achieving promotion to the old First Division. Which, in the manner of Geordies, they felt they had a natural right be part of. A right that, as they saw it, had been confounded for far too long by a pusillanimous board, fickle managers, witless players and mere bad luck.

The publicans of Tyneside could rest easy as the next two years would see countless drinks sunk in honour of the man who would be variously known as King Kev, Special K, KK and Wor Kev. Keegan wasn't trying to wrong-foot the Queen. He was genuinely not sure of what he wanted to do himself. And when it came to Newcastle United he never really would be.

His decision to retire as a player was one he would never fully work out, and one he would never fully revoke. It was one he was destined to remake and repent again and again. On this occasion he would put it off for long enough bring the Geordies what they wanted, though it was to prove to be the opening move in a relationship that was going to leave him grey-haired and with the psychological balance of a distressed Girl Guide.

Paradoxically it is the players who have achieved the most in football who are most likely to reject it in the end. It is the almost-beens, the Second Division sluggers and the low-waged utility men who cling on long after dignity demands or results excuse it. And, with a few very notable exceptions, most managers were not great players. But on the pitch Keegan had been amongst the achievers.

In 1982 few if any English players had achieved so much. Keegan's shopping list of personal triumph is well known, but perhaps underrated. Read it again and consider. Sixty-three full England caps, three League Championship medals, one FA Cup winner's medal, one European Cup winner's medal, two UEFA Cup winner's medals, one German Bundesliga medal, the Football Writers Association Player of the Year in 1976, the West German Footballer of the Year in 1978 and finally the European Footballer of the Year in 1978 and 1979. The fact that he won so many awards dependent on the votes of his peers and professional football writers gives away the secret of his success. Players and writers alike are impressed by natural talent and outrageous ability. However, footballers who aren't born with those abilities but who battle to success at the highest level by dint of their own ambition and personality, are even more respected. Keegan had got where he had the hard way. A skinny undersized youth who was overlooked by most of the talent spotters, Keegan achieved through application. Few players had worked quite so intensely.

Football is littered with stories of working-class lads who might not have lived in boxes and dined on lard and gravel but who certainly came from a straightened background. Jack and Bobby Charlton used to practise in the backyard using their dad's rolled-up pit socks for a ball, the young Don Revie played on the streets of Middlesbrough with a ball engineered from a bundle of rags. Keegan was brought up in and around the south Yorkshire town of Doncaster. His father, a miner from Hetton-le-Hole in County Durham, had migrated south after the War when work had become scarce in his native area.

Keegan junior experienced all the old-fashioned urban deprivation so popular with comedy sketch writers and romantic novelists. The family home was a traditional northern terrace. The toilet was outside and the bath, made of zinc, was kept in a cupboard. His father Joe had not enjoyed good breaks, he did his military service in the Far East, in a forgotten war against the Japanese, and caught malaria in the Burmese jungle in the process. Years down the pit had left him with diseased lungs and with the unquenchable resolve that his son would never go down a coal mine; he even refused to allow Keegan to go on a school trip to Markham Main Colliery. Joe wasn't a feckless man but, like many north-easterners, when he wasn't working he liked to sink some bitter and put a couple of quid on the horses, and as was the tradition and the norm in the North, his wife concentrated her energies on looking after their three children and keeping the family home together.

Keegan was a footballer from the word go, knocking a football against the garage doors of the funeral parlour across the road from his house. Eventually the Keegans moved to a cleaner, more modern estate next door to some playing fields and he was free to play on grass. A small boy but not overly skinny, he had to prevail against more muscular youths who would be quick to knock him off the ball. Initially he opted to play in goal but it soon became apparent that he would never be tall enough to be an effective goalkeeper. He changed position and as a midfielder learnt quickly not to back down in the face of intimidation. If anything he learnt the lesson too well. Although Keegan's mother Doris was a Protestant, his father was a Catholic and he was sent to a Catholic school where it was a nun who first noted he had the makings of a good player. When he wasn't playing extra football after school Keegan had time to fall victim to a strange accident that resulted in him biting his tongue off. But, as Alex Ferguson, Sky Sports, and several million startled viewers were to find out some time later, it was successfully sewn back on at the local hospital. Keegan was acutely aware of his diminutive stature, something that was emphasised to him when he was turned down for a job as a paper boy because he wasn't tall enough to reach the letter box. After a blow to the ego like that it wasn't long before he was working out at a boxing gym. But size continued to haunt Keegan.

Aged fifteen he was employed as the tea boy at a Doncaster factory on a weekly salary of £4.50. Even here he had trouble with getting in the team and Keegan was quite literally passed over in favour of a bigger man. As the selector put it, 'He was chosen because we needed a big lad. He was twice Keegan's size and we needed the extra weight.' A pattern was forming in Keegan's life and he was going to have to fight extra hard to achieve. Because of his size, the will to battle, even when there was no battle to be won, would never leave him.

While playing for Pegler Brass Works could drive some people crazy, especially if they were not getting an automatic game as Keegan wasn't, he persevered and kept his eyes on the prize, to sign professional forms for a league club. His abilities and his father's support and enthusiasm eventually earned Keegan trials with Doncaster Rovers and Coventry City. Like the paper shop, Coventry rejected Keegan on the grounds that he was too small. Meanwhile he was turning out for the Doncaster youth side and enduring countless Saturdays of physical intimidation. Keegan had started at the university of life, and was now firmly enroled in the school of hard knocks. His appearances were irregular for the factory team, but they were to prove of immense importance, for while slogging through the mud of municipal Doncaster pitches he was noticed by a scout for Scunthorpe United. As Keegan recalled, 'When I couldn't even get into the Pegler Brass Works first team my ambitions were in ruins, but I looked forward to playing with my mates in the local leagues at weekends. Then one game for a pub team called Lonsdale Hotel seemed just like any other. But it was to be the one that changed my life. My marker was a chap called Bob Nellis, a Scunthorpe scout who had been told to be on the look out for likely lads in the Doncaster area. I gave him the run around and he invited me to Scunthorpe for a trial. After six weeks I did well in a trial match and manager Ron Ashman asked me if I was interested in signing as an apprentice professional. I'd finally made it.'

Keegan signed for Scunthorpe in December 1968. Success is often built on lucky moments like Keegan's performance for a pub team. Keegan's way into the game could should inspire every seventeen-year-old who is struggling to get out of bed on Sunday morning to face some clod-hoppers on a windy moor or knee deep in a half-sunk swamp. Keegan had arrived and was understandably euphoric. But, as is euphoria's wont, it soon wore off.

Life at Scunthorpe was to be as unremittingly grim as the town's name suggests it should be. Soon enough Scunthorpe were demoted from the Third Division to the Fourth and Keegan found that his new career offered wages that were barely enough to cover his board and lodgings. Having left the brass works (who were less than chuffed by his decision to leave their team in the lurch) he found himself with little brass in his pocket. What he did have was a place to learn how to be a professional footballer and, just as importantly for his future in the game, it was the place where he developed his physique. The Fourth Division was no place for weaklings and before long Keegan was developing the barrel chest and muscular legs that would power his future performances. Keegan was fortunate to have Ashman as his first manager, a man who was considerate and protective of his charges and aware that Keegan was still in need of protection if he was going to survive for any length of time, and so dropped Keegan for games against the more physical teams. Keegan was only 17 and the Fourth Division had legions of hired assassins in their late twenties who would think nothing of removing a limb from any youngster who had the cheek to dance round them with the ball.

As a player Keegan developed very quickly, experiencing his first state of glory, albeit the Lincolnshire kind, when Sheffield Wednesday came to the Old Show Ground and Scunthorpe beat them 2-1.

If the past is another country, then Scunthorpe is Keegan's Outer Mongolia and looking back he lamented the fact that much of his early playing career is unrecorded.

'I scored, what 200 hundred league goals? I've only got about ten on tape. Most matches weren't even shown on television. Some of the great goals I scored, well, the cameras weren't there. Now every goal is shown even if you're a Third Division player, which is lovely. I'd love to see some of the goals I scored at Scunthorpe.'

During Keegan's stay at Scunthorpe from 1968 to 1971 he played in 124 matches, scoring eighteen of those goals that he would love to see now. However, the next goals Keegan was going to score would be in a very different arena. It was part of the appeal of English football that its leagues had room for small clubs who played on rough pitches watched by several hundred people in tin shacks as well as for city clubs with their immense stadiums and support. And where Keegan was headed was a truly immense destination.

Across the Pennines the brooding intelligence of Liverpool manager Bill Shankly had come to rest on the Scunthorpe player.

Shankly's friend and part-time scout for Liverpool, Andy Beattie, had been nagging the great man. As Shankly recalled in his auto-biography, 'The very first thing he said to me when he arrived was, "There is a boy at Scunthorpe. He is about eighteen. I have been watching him now for nine months. I think he has tremen-dous potential and I can't understand why nobody has gone for him."' Beattie kept on at Shankly who was by now aware that other clubs were interested in Keegan. He made his decision after watching Keegan play for Scunthorpe against Everton at Goodison Park.

Keegan arrived at Anfield from Scunthorpe for £33,000. Such was to be the success of the move that Shankly was later to call the deal 'robbery with violence' and suggest that Scunthorpe would have been perfectly justified in asking for another £100,000. By Shankly's own admission Keegan's purchase marked the foundation of his second great Liverpool team, a team whose inspiration would prove to be Keegan himself.

For Keegan it was the start of one of the defining relationships of his life. Both men had different memories of their early meet-ings. Shankly's was loaded with affection, 'We were in the Cup Final and the place [Anfield] was alive when Kevin arrived. He sat on top of a dustbin beside the temporary offices we had at Anfield while the new stand was being fitted out, and it must have seemed that nobody was taking any notice of him. He must have thought, "Christ, this is a place." But one fellow was taking notice of him, and that was me. I said, "Listen, son, you'll get your pants all dirty on that bin. Don't sit on dirty bins."' It was hard advice to fault. Shankly was the sort of man who could establish an immediate authority over a player's life by discussing their pants.

Keegan's memories are less concise, small wonder as the eighteen-year-old was probably in a whirl of disbelief at the time. 'Shankly had me hooked from the moment I set foot in Anfield. Nobody could give a guided tour with so much feeling. Even the most inconsequential item merited a glowing description in that unforgettable Scottish accent, "Look at this son... isn't it fantastic? Wouldn't you love to play here, son?", "The place heaves, son. They live, eat and sleep football", "We've got a great team son, great players, the best."' To Keegan's memory his manager called him son four times in three sentences. An appropriate memory, as Shankly was to become a father figure to Kevin.

But before he could learn to love the atmosphere of Anfield Keegan had to successfully negotiate the signing-on process, and in doing so he gave an early glimpse of the hard-nosed business man that was to emerge later. As Keegan recalled it was his father who had spurred him on to get the best deal he could. 'Before I left Scunthorpe with their manager Ron Ashman my dad had instructed me, "Don't sell yourself cheap." And I was a bit shocked when Bill Shankly started the discussions about my contract at Liverpool by offering me about £45 a week. It wasn't a lot more than I had been getting at Scunthorpe.

'I told him, "I'm sorry Mr Shankly but it isn't enough."

'I didn't con him. I stood my ground just on my father saying don't sell yourself cheap. But it was Ron Ashman I felt really sorry for because they offered £33,000 and that would be the equivalent of getting an offer of £400,000 or £500,000 now. For a

Fourth Division player as it then was it was unheard of. They'd agreed fees and it was a lifeline for Scunthorpe. I think they were going to spend some of the money on a stand and I think Ron Ashman nearly took a wobbler when I said no, he could see those £33,000 and lifeline suddenly drifting away. The minute he [Shankly] said, "Well how does £50 sound?" I said, "Well...fine." The point was made, now I could go back and tell my Dad that I'd squeezed another fiver out of the great Bill Shankly.

'The thing I learned from Shankly there was that although my basic was £50, my appearance was £70, so if I got into the first team I wasn't far behind Emlyn Hughes, Tommy Smith, Chris Lawler, Peter Thomson, Ron Yeats, all these people. That's something I've carried on and I've said, "Hold on, what's wrong with giving them a sensible wage but a really good incentive to get into the first team?" I'm a great believer in that; Shankly taught me that. I got straight into the team. So straight away from Scunthorpe, on nothing really, to that. They are little things you pick up that stand you in very good stead, now I think, "Yeah that's the way to do it."

'Every time I see a video of Shankly I get goose-pimples, because I thought so much of the man. It's nice to hear him speak again, I was a big fan of his, looked up to him and admired him. Whenever I do after-dinner speaking the speech is based on Bill Shankly and some of the great stories that are true, well 95 per cent true. Some of the things he said and did were so funny and yet so real, he was a very real person. There were no airs and graces with him and he didn't suffer fools. And his motivation, well, what is motivation? I remember when they signed Ron Yeats. Yeats was under the shower after he had done his medical and Shankly walked in and said, 'Come here boys, there he is, the man's a colossus, walk round him.' And about five journalists actually walked round him under the shower and got absolutely soaked. That's motivation, to just say and they do. I know how they felt. I think the last three caught on and didn't walk under, but he wouldn't have played them on the Saturday those three.'

Keegan's first season at Liverpool was proof of his ability. Happy playing from midfield or as a straight forward striker, he was utilised by Shankly as an attacking midfielder, and Keegan snatched the opportunity to excel. He started in the same way he would at Newcastle United eleven years later, by scoring in his opening match at home, helping Liverpool beat Nottingham Forest 3-1. Liverpool would win nothing in his first season, but Keegan established himself as an outstanding First Division player. Part of the reason for his success was his extreme physical fitness, the drive to make up for his height would now pay a dividend, as Keegan realised, 'When I went to Liverpool I was the fittest player there. It blew my mind yet it didn't really surprise me because I worked so hard on my fitness by doing weights and running up and down the cantilever steps of the stands. I used to run up and down behind one of the senior pros with a pair of dumbbells in my hands. All I knew was that this bloke had the best physique I'd seen in my life and I thought if he did that then I should too. In those days it was as simple as that. It was important being a small person playing up front that people could bounce off me sometimes. When I got to Liverpool I wasn't behind anyone, and I think the other lads respected that. They thought, "This lad can run. He's got stamina and speed."'

It's the eternal mystery of Keegan's career that the very stamina that established him as a player and forged him as a man should fail him when he later came to press for the Championship as a manager. He had shown so much commitment as a player that the suspicion remains that he had invested too much of his own drive; so later in life, when he turned to the role of manager, he would find that there was none left.

More importantly in his early days at Liverpool he quickly cemented his relationship with Shankly. In the UEFA Cup of 1972/73 Keegan found himself playing in Europe. Just over a year after leaving Scunthorpe's Old Show Ground he was scoring the first of Liverpool's two goals against Eintracht Frankfurt in the first round of the competition. Domestically Liverpool started that season by beating both Manchester City and Manchester United 2-0 and from then on they were always the likely Champions. In only his second season at Anfield Keegan had gained a Champions medal with a UEFA Cup winner's medal to follow when Liverpool beat Borussia Mönchengladbach. Keegan scored twice in the 3-0 home-leg victory. Not only had he achieved that, but he had established a winning partnership with the tall Welsh striker John Toshack, yet another man who would be amongst the favourites years later to replace Keegan as the manager of Newcastle United. Despite the closeness of his relationship with Shankly, Keegan was always likely to display his tendency to walk away if his commitment or honesty was questioned. On one occasion Keegan complained of having a sore foot, a genuine injury that had been caused by the over-stiff clutch of his car, but as far as Shankly was concerned Keegan was trying it on, and whilst Keegan was receiving electrolysis treatment he told him so: 'He reached down, ripped off one of the electrodes and shouted, "There's nothing wrong with you. You're playing." Keegan, convinced that Shankly was calling him a cheat, responded hotly, 'I'm not being called that. If you want me you'll find me at my parents' home in Doncaster.' It was a reaction the football world, and the supporters and staff of Newcastle United, would come to know well. Then Joe Keegan was still alive and when his son turned up in Yorkshire and told him what had happened he sent him straight back to Merseyside. Shankly didn't hold grudges, especially as he was usually the victor, and Keegan stayed to be part of that great side.

A major factor behind Liverpool's success was the consistency of team selection, with pretty much the same players turning out each week. The continuity bred confidence which ultimately led to victory. Yet like so much that Keegan is widely believed to have learnt from the master, this failed to lodge in Keegan's mind. Or if it did he forgot it. Consistency was one of Shankly's most central ethics yet one his pupil was to jettison in the future in his relentless search for the ultimate attacking team.

The next season brought mixed success for Shankly, Liverpool and Keegan. There was disappointment when they were knocked out of the European Cup by Red Star Belgrade and beaten to the League Championship by Don Revie's Leeds United, but also joy when they won the FA Cup. Although the final against Newcastle United was a triumph for Keegan – he scored twice – the day saw the seeds sown of his eventual decision to leave Liverpool. After forty years in football Bill Shankly chose the day that Keegan destroyed Newcastle United to end his time at Liverpool. As the players came out of the showers at Wembley, Shankly sat with a cup of tea and a pie and quietly decided that he had come to the end of his time at the club. Amid the euphoria of the moment only one player noticed something different about the boss. As Shankly remarked, 'Kevin Keegan sensed my feelings then. He said so later.'

On July 12, 1974, the decision was made public by Liverpool chairman John Smith at a press conference to announce the arrival of Ray Kennedy from Arsenal. Quite simply Shankly had had enough. 'I had been around a long time and I thought I would like to have a rest, spend more time with my family and maybe get a bit more fun out of life. Whilst you love football, it is a hard relentless task which goes on and on like a river. There is no time for stopping and resting. So I had to say I was retiring. That's the only word for it, thought I believe you retire when you're in a coffin and the lid is nailed down and your name is on it.' Shankly had been at Anfield for 15 years and won much. When Keegan left Newcastle he would have been there for five years and won little. However the reasoning of the men was very similar.

At the time Keegan was devastated by the loss of Shankly and although he had guessed something was amiss, when he heard the news it still didn't make sense. 'I was absolutely shattered when I heard he had resigned. I was at Manchester Airport, just back from a holiday when one of the of the porters rushed over. "Seen the news about Shanks?" he said. I hadn't a clue, but my first thought was that he was dead or maimed in a car crash.

Resigned. I couldn't believe it. I always thought they'd find him in years to come slumped over his desk.'

Speaking in 1984 Keegan was still troubled by the loss of his mentor. 'Shankly's decision to quit staggered me. To this day I can't understand why he did it. And I was as close to him as anyone but when I heard about it my first reaction was sheer disbelief. I wondered what he was going to do. He couldn't just sit at home and do nothing, and managing any other club than his beloved Liverpool was out of the question. I wanted to leave that year, really, but I had made a deal with Mr Smith.' Keegan's memories of Shankly's departure are as revealing of the player as they are of his manager. Even at a club as big and as successful as Liverpool Keegan wanted to walk out, an instinct that seemed to set itself against all the tenacity and staying power he had shown to get from Peglers Brass Works to Anfield in the first place.

At the end of the 1975/76 season Keegan was ready to move on. His England career was blooming. In 1972 Sir Alf Ramsey gave Keegan his international debut against Wales. In 1974 Don Revie took the England job and a year later Keegan was dropped for the 20 May match against Wales again. Keegan had taken the decision badly, leaving the squad headquarters in a huff and failing to watch the game. He claimed 'It's the end of my international career.' Which, of course, it wasn't. Four days later he was recalled by Revie for England against Scotland. England won 5-1. A year later Revie made Keegan captain.

For a young man Keegan was very astute in knowing how to advance his career. If Keegan wanted to crown his glory he would have to move and he knew where to. Keegan was off to Europe. At the start of the 1976/77 season he made his feelings known to the club and like a good team man he went first to the manager Bob Paisley. But Paisley, a shy product of the Durham coal field, wasn't at home with talk of transfers and Europe. He was still feeling his way in to the position of manager and his mind was on football and nothing else. Paisley would become the most successful manager in the history of English football, but when Keegan approached him he told him not to talk to him about it but to the chairman. Keegan was astounded by what he saw as an abdication of responsibility. That a manager should not be willing to talk about the transfer of one of his best players was beyond his comprehension, and consequentially his relations with Paisley would never be completely happy. When Keegan approached the board he did so with a strong hand, having been indirectly approached by Real Madrid and other European sides who were interested in signing him. As reigning Champions Liverpool were in the European Cup, and if Paisley had seemed unconcerned about Keegan's departure John Smith certainly wasn't.

The fact that Keegan stayed was mainly due to financial inducement. The deal he made with Smith guaranteed that his sale fee would be fixed at £500,000 if he remained to the end of the season. That season was to be one of his greatest as a player though his popularity on the terraces was affected by his public admission that he intended to depart Anfield: 'By next summer I expect to have left Anfield and start another life abroad – possibly in Spain.'

Keegan had already proved himself to possess a typically Yorkshire ability to amass extra cash. As well as his burgeoning media work he was involved in lucrative sponsorship deals, and the word on Merseyside was that he was becoming a greedy man who was only in it for the money. Given that not many people on Merseyside would have had a background as hard as his, it was an unfair judgement. Like Don Revie he wasn't greedy per se, he'd just seen enough of poverty in his youth to want to make very sure that he never went back there and that his family never had to experience it. There is an inverted snobbery in this country that resents footballers making lots of money, as if a man who makes his way by dint of his physical labour should not be greatly rewarded. Few supporters complain about the inherited wealth of many of the upper-class men who are the chairmen at clubs. Keegan was sensitive to the accusations, 'People who know me well realise, I'm sure, that there is much more to me than just money. For instance, I would never have asked Liverpool for a testimonial. I just don't think that players who are as well paid as I am are entitled to one. They should be reserved for the less well-off in lower divisions. No, money doesn't rule my life. I want the things it can buy, but basically I'm the type of person who can never be content to stay put.'

Keegan was constantly connected with continental teams; at one point he looked certain to go to Italy but changed his mind although, as he recalls, the decision was made for him. 'I didn't decide that I wouldn't go to Italy, my wife decided that I wouldn't go to Italy. I don't forget that, I'm not one for regrets, I've had no regrets over any move I've ever done. People said I was wrong to leave Liverpool when I did. My point was that it was time to go. There is a time to come and a time to go. It was probably me just making football the master, that was where I was wrong. The moral of that story really is that I had gone a long way down the line, not committed myself, but almost committed myself verbally to going to a club without consulting the main person in my life and the one which it would affect most, which was my wife. And, to be fair to her, although she's never ever interfered in football, never said I don't want to go to Newcastle, I want to stay here, on this particular occasion, because at the time kidnapping was rife in Italy, and what you have got to remember is a woman thinks differently to a man (and we all find that out to our cost sometimes), she just said no, and I think that she was right and that I was wrong.'

Aware that he intended to go, the supporters lost some of their enthusiasm for Keegan. They resented his decision and were unable to understand why anyone would wish to play for any other side in the world. Surely Liverpool were the greatest?

That last season proved the supporters right. Liverpool won the Championship again, only losing out on the double when they were beaten 2-1 by Manchester United in the FA Cup Final. To a large degree it was Keegan who did it for them. Liverpool's supreme moment in 1977 was beating Borussia Mönchengladbach 3-1 in the European Cup Final. Keegan's last game for Liverpool wasn't blessed by a goal, but his personal performance set the tenor of the game. So nimble was he that the great German international Berti Vogts was reduced to bringing him down in the area for a penalty. Phil Neal's resulting spot-kick deciding the match.

Keegan was now one of the biggest names in world football,

and more importantly he was a free man. But it would be some time before he could spend as much time in Spain as he would have liked. Keegan was going to Germany. Bob Paisley made no serious attempt to keep him at the club, but maybe the un-assuming Durham man had just been canny enough to have been already eyeing a replacement for Keegan: Celtic's Kenny Dalglish. If Keegan had been great for Liverpool, Dalglish would be better.

Part of Kevin Keegan had left with Bill Shankly. 'The fans thought I went to Hamburg for the money, but Liverpool died for me the day my idol quit.' It was typical of Keegan that he should lament the personality of Shankly, who won compara-tively little compared to his successor. Keegan was overtly emo-tional in public about Shankly's departure: 'Bill Shankly was my idol at Anfield. To me he was Liverpool. Liverpool died for me when Shankly left. I would never have contemplated playing anywhere else while he was there. Without him the club was never quite the same. I have a lot of respect for Bob Paisley, I like him as a friend and he is someone I can confide in. But he will never fill the gap in my life that Shankly left. Nobody could.' He sounded like a man reading the service at his wife's funeral.

'Without Bill's guidance, advice and encouragement, I could never have achieved what I did in the game.

'People told me I was mad to leave Liverpool. Occasionally I've thought it would be good to be like Ian Callaghan and stay with one club, but to do this I'd have to wear blinkers and keep along the one course. It's not for me.

'It annoys me slightly when people ask, "Don't you think you owe Liverpool something?" I don't owe Liverpool anything.'

'I've known the agony'

Keegan was signed by West German club SV Hamburg for £500,000 in June 1977. Once more Keegan scored in his opening match, a pre-season friendly against Barcelona at SV Hamburg's Volkspark ground. If he had been less than popular with Scousers of late, he was immediately confirmed as a favourite of the German crowd, scoring in the 6-0 defeat of a side that included Johan Cruyff. When he first arrived at Hamburg the management team of Peter Krohn and Rudi Gutendorf were somewhat confused as to how best utilize Keegan. The side finished only 10th in the Bundesliga; and it would not be until the next season and the arrival of Gunter Netzer as manager, and trainer Branco Zebec, that Keegan would fully develop into the best player in Europe. At the time Keegan made it clear about where and how he expected to play, 'Actually I like to be given a free role, and be able to play where I think I can have my best game. If I feel I can do better on the wing I'd like to be able to play there. The worst thing a coach can say to me is to do a certain thing, or play in a certain position. The best thing he can say is to tell me to play my own game.'

The same concerns that some in Liverpool had expressed about Keegan's alleged greed were now emerging amongst certain members of the Hamburg squad. From the moment that he had arrived in Germany, hardly an inch of his body wasn't covered in a Keegan-endorsed item of clothing. He was reputed to have made thousands personally from the transfer deal and he was also regarded as being stand-offish by players who were, not to put too fine a point on it, jealous. Kevin Keegan had it all.

Such was his appeal to German youth that the West German Federal Government used him to advertise the importance of voting in the European elections. That campaign was such a success that he was employed to promote fuel and energy conservation. This involved a cartoon strip in which two space travellers pondered, 'The humans have energy problems. We must suggest to the inhabitants of Earth that they think more positively about energy wastage. That means work for our best man...SUPER KEVIN.' On this cue the cartoon image of Keegan as Superman appeared. His catchphrase was 'I'm already on my way, Master', and he went on to break up a bemused teenage party, whose occupants had been stupid enough to leave the windows open and let all of the heat out. As far as Keegan was concerned he was maximising his potential and, as he later told *Goal*, he always kept his mind on football.

'The only contract that ever mattered was my contract to play football and I never lost sight of that. If I was playing well for Liverpool or Hamburg or Southampton and England, then people want to be associated with you, for shin pads, aftershave, all sorts of things, just to have that association with what they feel is a mass audience, people who watch football. I didn't find it any problem at all. A journalist once tried to say that I did too much, but I said the time to criticise is when I can't do it on the football field, you can do it then, but while I'm still doing well you can't. I think that it actually helped me. I don't think I was paranoid, I was just obsessed with football. Suddenly to go and do a picture session for say Fabergé or some new boots that we had designed was a relief, a release if you like from every day talking football, eating, sleeping and drinking football, and I think in some ways that helped me because it kept me fresh. I thought I must play well on a Saturday otherwise they'll say that because I went for a picture shoot on Thursday afternoon that was why I didn't play well. It put a little bit more pressure on you to play well, but if you are that type of person and you respond to it, then in many ways it helps you too.

'You do tend to pick up stuff and you get a lot of sports gear given to you. Some of the stuff, to be fair, you never wear because it's not you, but the people want to give it to you and it would be wrong not to give it to you. The guest bathroom had a bit of Brut in it and the downstairs loo had some in. I've still got a lot of the stuff. We did bedroom slippers with my name on, they did rugs with my picture where kids could come and wipe their feet, I don't know what they were trying to tell me there. I kept them because my kids didn't see it when I played football, they only see it on video and they laugh at the hairstyles that I have had that were in at the time, like the feather cut, when I used to run down the wing it was like an aeroplane, my hair used to come out like two wings, a lot of people thought that was where I got my speed from. The kids laugh at it now, but at the time you did follow fashion and clothes. Video has been a terrible thing for people like me; you can say to kids I was very trendy but they can see what you looked like. They can see the 20-inch flares and the stuff that you thought you looked the bees knees in, but fashion has just beaten me now. Having been out of the game for eight years I go to grounds now and people produce photographs I've never seen and when the lads see them, especially the ones from my Scunthorpe days, they just kill themselves. They see the Liverpool ones with the hair and some of the modelling I did at the time, which are now very dated, and they have a habit of passing them around the Newcastle bus and having a giggle about them. I say to them, you'll be doing the same in 20 years time. If you are successful you'll be looking at a contract you had and a session you had where you thought you looked great and in 20 years time you will be cringing.'

Keegan also had the answer to the jealousy at Hamburg – he became the ultimate club player. But he was never to win the friendship of his team-mates. The arrival of his previous adversary from Borussia Mönchengladbach, Zebec, was to be his making. Most importantly it would convince England manager Ron Greenwood of Keegan's worth. Keegan's season didn't start brightly, and it wasn't until his twelfth match for Hamburg, that he scored his first Bundesliga goal. At the next game a crowd of 61,000 saw him score twice in the 4-2 home victory over Schalke.

Keegan got his way, and was allowed to roam the field and, with a team that included such players as Manny Kaltz, Rudi Kargus, Jimmy Hartwig and Horst Hrubesch, Hamburg became a winning side. Despite losing 1-2 at home to Bayern Munich in the last game of the season, it was too late for anyone to catch them. The gamble had paid off, and Keegan was a West German Championship winner, scoring 17 league goals in the process.

1978 also saw the permanently aggrieved bantam-weight that lurks in Keegan's soul make itself known again. In a regional derby match against Lübeck, Keegan, tired of the over attentive and at times downright illegal marking of Erhard Preuss, reacted in a manner witnessed once before, at the 1974 Charity Shield. That time Keegan and Billy Bremner traded blows on their way to the tunnel after being sent-off. The clash with Bremner had been a playground tussle but in Lübec Keegan laid out his opponent with a carefully judged right-hander. The punch was quickly followed by an eight-match ban.

By the summer of 1978 the attitude of the other Hamburg players became both untenable for Keegan and unbelievable for onlookers. The breaking point came in a friendly match at Real Madrid in Spain which Hamburg won 4-2. But the main cause of wonder to the 80,000 spectators was the refusal of Keegan's teammates to pass the ball to him. When Keegan arrived in Madrid the press had been out in force, fêting him like royalty, and by comparison the rest of the Hamburg squad had been ignored – they took their revenge on the pitch and after the match Keegan was furious, asking if the fans could believe it either. 'Is that the former captain of England out there? They couldn't have believed what they saw. That wasn't me, it was a running "dummy" who was hardly offered the ball. I'm a key player and ask to be treated like one. I've experienced a lot of frustration because I'm not accepted on the field by my team-mates as I should be. I refuse to be thought of as the nice Englishman who died a death. And that's what I'd be doing if I stayed here.'

Even by Keegan's high standards of fraught public confessional this was quite an outburst. And once he started, like a drunk teenager who finally lets his mum and dad know how he feels, he couldn't stop. 'I would like to join Real Madrid and see if I can find the dream I'm chasing. I want to find the dream I'm chasing. I want to find something with total job satisfaction – I'm not chasing a pot of gold. I 've kept a lot of this inside me but I cannot hold it any more.' If that sounds familiar it's almost word for word what Keegan said in his infamous outburst against Alex Ferguson on Sky TV. Keegan, the man willing to fool about for the camera, to ape Charlie Chaplin on his return to Doncaster so his mates didn't think he'd got above himself just because he was in the money, the man willing to take part in the most asinine of photo-opportunities, was showing the split personality that would later define his relationship with Newcastle United.

Keegan had two reactions to stress, he would either lash out with his fists, or publicly lament, almost tearfully, the terrible situation he was in. It wasn't, of course, that terrible a situation. He was by now awash with money and in January 1979 was awarded the European Footballer of the Year (1978). But even that was not an unblemished achievement, the respected journal *World Soccer* commenting, 'Keegan during the past year has established himself as perhaps the No.1 personality in the Bundesliga and his displays in the European Championship for England have demonstrated that he truly ranks among the outstanding players in Europe and the world...but...after all, what did Keegan win in 1978? Not the West German League, not the cup, no European title and he didn't appear in the World Cup Finals.' In August 1979 Hamburg and Keegan did win something: they became Bundesliga champions.

It has been suggested that Keegan's outbursts are well judged ploys rather than uncontrollable displays of emotion. But if that particular display was meant to encourage his swift conversion to life as a Spanish footballer it didn't work. Keegan remained in Germany until 1980. However, if it was meant to improve his terms and conditions, then perhaps it was a carefully judged gamble. A week later Keegan hadn't only calmed down, he was if anything, quite chipper. But ever the philosophical brooder, he said, 'I've had a terrible caning from the German press though some remarks were grossly unfair. I've had a tense two-hours-and-ten-minutes talk with our manager Gunter Netzer, and no punches were pulled. I've had some pain. I've known the agony and I'm pleased now that it's all out in the open.' The pain and agony weren't so great though as to stop him from making an exact calculation of how long the meeting lasted. Perhaps it was in those vital last ten minutes that Keegan got exactly what he wanted from Netzer. 'Some good came from the wreckage. I have come to an agreement with Gunter Netzer which must remain secret but I'm much happier now than I was before.' Before anyone came to the obvious conclusion, Keegan added the caveat, 'I'm not chasing money. I just want to be remembered as an honest guy who earned his corn.'

None the less, by the time Keegan left Hamburg he was earning a fortune. His actual annual wage from Hamburg was £150,000, but extras were netting him a further £500,000 a year. British Petroleum were paying him £125,000 a year, on top of that he endorsed Patrick football boots, advertised milk on television, could earn the best part of £3,500 an hour at autograph sessions and was a regular studio guest for the BBC.

Keegan had signed a three-year contract for Hamburg and it was a time scale he intended to stick to. Although Hamburg had been beaten by Nottingham Forest in that year's European Cup Final, by 1980 there was little more Keegan felt he could achieve in Germany. His daughter, Laura Jane, born in 1978, had suffered health problems and his wife was by now ready to take the family back to England. For all the interest of big clubs in England there was one small First Division club that offered Keegan a stage on which he would surely shine and easy access to the horse racing world of which he was so enamoured. Manager Lawrie McMenemy signed Keegan for Southampton for £400,000.

Keegan's agent Harry Swales, barely able to conceal the purr in the back of his throat, commented, 'Kevin appreciates more than anyone that everything he has is down to football. If he wasn't at the top in football, these companies wouldn't want him and employ him. He won't be taking on more than is good for him. He won't be jet-setting about all over the place. Lawrie McMenemy and I are old friends. I handled Southampton's pool in the 1976 Cup Final. There won't be any problems.'

But there were. Almost from the beginning of his time on the south coast Keegan became injury prone and he was also to fall out with the Geordie manager at the club, Lawrie McMenemy. Although Lawrie McMenemy was a friend of Keegan's, it wasn't feelings of regional pride or bonhomie that facilitated Keegan's move to Newcastle after two years at the Dell.

McMenemy had created a side on the south coast that had reached the top part of the First Division, and who looked capable of winning the Championship and qualifying for Europe. The team was built around three England players: Alan Ball, Mick Channon and Kevin Keegan. All three were convinced that just one more buy on McMenemy's behalf would be enough to secure the Championship. To Keegan this was such an obvious fact that he repeatedly asked his manager to go ahead and do it. However Keegan's repeated demands led to stress in their relationship, which finally manifested itself after a 0-3 home defeat to Aston Villa in which Keegan's efforts were conspicuous by their absence. But he still felt the match had proved his point. Before he could get the words out McMenemy turned on him, saying, 'You can keep quiet. You cheated today.'

This was a time in Keegan's life when the public perception of him was still that of a permanently smiling, even slightly gormless figure, yet the same anger lurked in him then that we have all come to know since. For a manager to call one of his players a cheat comes fairly high up the list of ways to get rid of them. If it was a deliberate plan, it worked. If it wasn't, it was a massive error of judgement from McMenemy. The reaction was instantaneous, as Keegan blurted, 'I just told him, "That's it I'm finished," and walked out.'

Nevertheless, a decade later Keegan was able to look back at his time at Southamptom with some warmth. 'I have no regrets about my time at Southampton. It would have been nice to do it with a small club, and we were very close to pinching the league. There were better teams around but for a season we played football that they still talk about down there; you know it was dream stuff, and it was because we had the players. The players now have to live with that down their throats all the time, people saying, "Oh, remember in the eighties, what a team that was between 1980 and 1982: Ball, Channon, Keegan. We had some characters there." It was great that it happened to Southampton. Yet at the end of that you realise why Southampton won't win the league, why they can't compete with Manchester United, Liverpool, Arsenal, Spurs and the big clubs. Southampton are not a big club. They hang in there and that's to the credit of the chairman, the managers and the players, but like the other smaller clubs, in reality they are looking for scraps off the table.

'At the start of the season Shankly used to have all the teams up on the wall, and there was really only us and Leeds then that mattered, and he'd say "There they are, boys. These two want to win it and these 20-odd want to stay in it." And that's how it was and he was right. It didn't mean to say that they wouldn't beat you sometimes, it didn't mean to say that they wouldn't beat you twice on the trot. But at the end of the day only two of us could win it and the rest were trying to survive in it. I think he summed it up in a nutshell. It's a bit different now, there's a great levelling out. It would be a little fairy tale if one of the smaller clubs could win it now and again, just to prove that you can't buy success in football, but I fear it won't happen. The big boys will just edge them out.'

Keegan would do a lot more walking in the future, but in the meantime the Newcastle manager, Arthur Cox, had his opportunity. Cox had already approached Keegan's agent Harry Swales earlier in the year. The usual secret meeting was arranged. Conveniently the club was, as it is now, sponsored by the Newcastle Breweries, and it was in one of their Swallow Hotels in London that the deal was done. The Newcastle team were nervous. Keen to leave no avenue of emotional pressure untapped they even told Keegan that one of their negotiators, Alistair Wilson, had left his family holiday in order to be there. Keegan recalled the supposedly family-deprived Wilson as being in 'a cold sweat'. It was a waste of sweat. Keegan was going to sign anyway.

There would be no problem leaving Southampton now. McMenemy had lost his working relationship with Keegan. As long as Keegan stayed, McMenemy's authority was challenged. It wasn't cynical, merely practical to let Keegan go, and although a good judge of horse flesh, McMenemy may well have made the mistake of thinking Keegan wouldn't get his form back. Keegan had become more accident prone of late, picking up hamstring injuries and, on one occasion, a ten-inch gash that ran the length of his shin. More importantly he had what was by his own lofty standards a disastrous World Cup campaign in Spain. The personal nadir of the competition was missing an open goal, a goal that would have kept England in the World Cup. Besides that McMenemy knew Keegan was right, he needed another player. But he would have to sell Keegan to get him.

Manchester United had expressed interest in Keegan, but he was wise to what was achievable. At Old Trafford he would need to shine brightly in order to achieve, at St James' Park he could just trot round the pitch and he would still be providing better fayre than the Newcastle supporters were used to. What's more the money, as they say, was good.

Keegan and Swales contrived to negotiate a deal where he got a share of the gate receipts at St James' Park, a brilliantly simple way to earn a lot. There was little danger of him losing his will to play whilst he kept the crowds coming in. They did come too, with Keegan adding an estimated extra 10,000 to the average attendance. When he left Newcastle he calculated that the deal had made him on average £3,000 a week. No other player was making that much in 1982.

Once Keegan had signed, Newcastle went insane.

'Life is about people'

Keegan's paternal grandfather, Frank, had achieved local fame in County Durham in 1909. He was amongst 26 miners who were trapped underground when the West Stanley pit was rocked by an explosion. Although 168 men died in the disaster, Keegan's grandfather had the clearness of mind to lead the other 25 men to safety. Keegan was connected at a very deep level with the people he was to live and work amongst. Pit disasters litter the folk memory of the north-east. They weren't just a distant horror from the old vicious days of private mine ownership (days that are back now with the engineered demise of the nationalised coal industry), they happened after the War as well. They were fresh memories that bonded people together, and Keegan knew the strengths of that culture but he also knew its weaknesses, a realisation that had driven him throughout his professional career. 'My dad was a typical miner. He went down the pit, worked hard, came up, had a beer, a bet on the horses and some Woodbines, then went back down again. Half the house was on cigarette coupons, the clock on the wall, the ducks and the wastepaper bins. He always said he was smoking to get things for the house. He died of cancer at 71. I want to achieve something in my life.'

In 1982, Newcastle was still going through the death throes of de-industrialisation. To other parts of England, the parts where Thatcherite morality had taken hold of the consciousness of the population, nostalgic talk of coalfields and shipyards and steel mills, all of which belonged to a dismissed past, were more redolent of a Monty Python sketch than anything that might be relevant to modern England. But in the north-east, they remained woven into the fabric of life. Although the superstructure had gone, the slag heaps grassed over, the shipyards decommissioned and the mills quiet, the class consciousness those industries created remains to this day. Not as an active commitment to socialism particularly – that is as discredited a word in the north-east as it is anywhere, if for different reasons. Nor in any sepia-tinted, flat-capped imagery (although Keegan keeps a sepia photograph of his grandfather Frank in full pit gear and flat cap on his mantelpiece) – people there dress in the same disconsolate American leisure-wear that the rest of the western world has fallen prey to, and live in the same faceless Barrett houses that clutter the rest of England. But they share an unfashionable and unbreakable pleasure in doing things together. It can be seen in the social clubs, in the packed streets of the Bigg Market on a Saturday night after a match, and most importantly in the football club. And if the football club was created by the enthusiasm of the industrial workers, it had, in turn, done them the favour of being the last great vestige of those times. Newcastle United is the past, a huge them-against-us representation of what Geordies can achieve en masse.

No matter how popular the game becomes in the sitting rooms of Hampshire or how many Sussex children turn away from the dismal huffing and puffing of Rugby Union in favour of a game of true grace as personified by players like David Ginola, no matter how many seats are installed in grounds or how smoothly transatlantic FA spokesman may become, the central nature of Association Football in this country cannot be changed. In essence it is a northern working-class game. It centres on the Pennine cities and the Clyde, the Tyne and the Mersey. And Keegan came face to face with that in his first cathartic match at St James' Park.

From the moment he took to the grass the ramshackle stadium echoed to his name. Keegan had never experienced such personal deification before. When he had moved from Scunthorpe and arrived as a player at Liverpool in 1971 he had only been 20 years old, brought in as a kid with prospects. Shankly expected Keegan to work his way into the unit. Shankly didn't like stars, he liked teams. Keegan had gradually developed into the consciousness of the Kop; he was respected at Liverpool, cherished even, but never idolised. Throughout his last season at Anfield Keegan's relationship with the Liverpool supporters had been compromised by his declaration at the start that he intended to leave at some point. Liverpool was a fiercely level place then, no one was allowed to be greater than the side and heads were regularly checked for bigness. The Liverpool supporters have only really worshipped one player in the last 20 years and that, ironically, was Kenny Dalglish, a man who was to make a career out of stepping into Keegan's shoes.

Newcastle United supporters funnel all their colossal passion and collective need through the conduit of individual players. So enamoured of stars are they that they will place figures as unlikely as Micky Quinn, the overweight Scouse goal machine that wore the Newcastle number nine shirt from 1989 to 1992, on a pedestal. Proud to be foot soldiers, they are born to be lead. And Keegan became the leader the moment he stepped out on to the pitch against Queens Park Rangers. These occasions invariably follow a plot progression so corny that it would embarrass Walt Disney. August 28, 1982 was such a day. St James' Park was, in the parlance of the local press, 'packed to the rafters' and as Keegan came out on to the field his name was chanted by 36,185 voices (minus the odd 400 or so who had struggled up from west London). It was an awesome welcome, and a crowd that wouldn't be bettered that season in the league. On the day Newcastle beat QPR 1-0 and Keegan scored the goal. He was immediately engulfed in the Gallowgate end. The Newcastle United supporters took Kevin Keegan to their heart that day, and at one point it looked like he mightn't emerge from the manic throng that had taken him in. The Gallowgate, a steep bank of concrete steps on the side of the ground that faces the Tyne, had derived its ghoulish name from the town's previous habit of dispatching felons in that area. It was a name that had recently been more appropriate than at any time since the last public execution, since many Newcastle sides had been good for nothing more than hanging.

By the time Keegan emerged from the manic throng his messiah status had been confirmed. He was genuinely moved by the reception, and he was as quick to admit as much to the press, 'I've seen it all...but playing before thousands of passionate Geordies will equal everything in my life.' If your life has already featured winning the European Cup that is quite a compliment. Now he was left with the small matter of providing some return on the emotional investment that the city had made in him.

Newcastle had finished ninth, eleventh and ninth in the Second Division in the previous three seasons. A record of unparalleled ordinariness. In recent history Newcastle had only threatened to win a trophy on two occasions. The last time had been in 1976 when Newcastle had been beaten 2-1 by Manchester City in the League Cup final, falling victim to the usual inspired performance from an exiled Geordie, in that case Dennis Tueart who scored with a phenomenal over-head kick. Two years before that Newcastle had reached the FA Cup final, a trophy which they had won six times and which was commonly held by Geordies to be their property, property which just happened to be on temporary loan to all the other teams that unlike them had won it in the modern era. They lost, well, no, they didn't lose, since they didn't actually play; they just sat back and watched the Liverpool number seven take them apart. Liverpool's number seven on that day was Kevin Keegan.

Of the two Liverpool goals he scored, Keegan was particulary pleased with the opener: 'Tommy Smith, what a storming game he had, centred, Brain Hall ducked, and there I was on the edge of the box ready, willing and able to drive the ball past Ian

McFaul into the right-hand top corner of the goal!' Steve Heighway had scored the second, leaving it to Keegan to finish Newcastle off. 'A few minutes from time with Newcastle fading fast, Tommy Smith and Stevie performed a couple of defence-wrecking one-twos, Tommy crossed the ball low and hard and there was yours truly on the far post to right-foot it home.' (The somewhat breathless tone of the prose is because by even that fairly early point in his career, Keegan was media-wise enough to be writing his own column for *Shoot* magazine.)

It was a cup final that made a mockery of the term mismatch. Keegan particularly remembered the lap of honour with the trophy. 'We stopped briefly in front of the Newcastle fans. Personally I would have spent more time with them.' Which, of course, was exactly what he was destined to do.

The Geordies trooped off home that day with nothing more than the usual accolades for being fantastic fans. Being called fantastic is not a substitute for winning, not for long anyway. Newcastle had been bought off for too long with admiration for its fervent support. The standard sports feature-writer's pay-off line was, 'Imagine what they would be like if they win something?' It's a comment on the effectiveness of Keegan's time as manager at Newcastle that a different generation of journalists would trot out the same cliché again.

But in 1982 it looked like that was all over. Keegan's arrival was the usually messianic affair that Tyneside withholds from all but favoured footballers. 'I'm now with United and we have to turn our potential into reality, but I've been here long enough to appreciate just what can happen if we give Geordie supporters a successful Second Division team, never mind one competing at the top of the first. I am staggered by the numbers we have had to see us this season. Sometimes I think they are too easily pleased, but I love their loyalty to a club that has had so little real success for so many years. I've played at the top for Liverpool and it's just like being on the summit of a glass mountain. Finish second and you're on the slide. Up here on Tyneside they don't have the one problem that worries virtually every other club in the league – lack of support. Life is about people and I am surrounded by some of the nicest people imaginable. I'll be here next season. I'll finish my playing career with Newcastle United, in perhaps a couple of years, and I've no ambition to become a manager.'

Although Terry McDermott had returned to Newcastle from Anfield to rejoin Keegan, it became apparent that Keegan alone would not be able to save Newcastle. A team would have to be built round him if the club were to have any chance of promotion. Apart from the cold realisation of what was possible on the pitch, Keegan the man was coming under closer scrutiny. Only a month after he had been called 'Britain's finest football ambassador', unease at his plethora of sponsorship deals was translated into criticism in the press. The *News of the World* opined, 'There is a body of opinion that says Keegan is in danger of tripping over his own ego as he runs out in his Patrick boots.' Accusations of greed were flying again, notably over his decision to leave Southampton whilst still under contract. He had been the first millionaire footballer and the suggestion was that money was his only motivation; again Keegan seethed, telling journalist Terry McNeil, 'Five years ago I was being cited as an example to the younger generation of footballers. It was said that I could conduct myself properly and that unlike a few others we could all name, I hadn't wasted my money, but invested it wisely. Now I'm being accused of making money. My God, the envy is simply incredible. Bitterness doesn't come into it, but I know that had I gambled away my money away, been a boozer and was on my third marriage I would be better thought of than I am now.'

Keegan's case was further complicated by two incidents that nearly lost him his sight. Playing in a testimonial match at Middlesbrough, an innocuous challenge resulted in an elbow going into his eye and damaging his retina. The injury was serous enough to put him in hospital. He missed eight matches, matches that Newcastle could ill afford to lose him for. Once he was fit to play again, Newcastle and Keegan travelled to Leeds for a league fixture. Elland Road, noted for the ferocity of the home supporters even at the most benign of times, proved particularly hostile on this occasion, as a Leeds fan catapulted a bolt at Keegan, missing his eye by inches. Keegan was poleaxed by the force of the blow, sinking to his knees in the penalty area.

Arthur Cox was wise to bring in the midfielder Terry McDermott. McDermott had played for Newcastle before; he had been a part of the 1974 FA Cup side that Keegan had demolished. But the more important factor was not McDermott's affinity for the club he had once served but his personal regard for Kevin Keegan, a regard that would later develop into devotion.

Gradually Newcastle's form picked up. The young winger Chris Waddle, who had promised much but whose hunched demeanour and hint of diminished effort had threatened to let him down, developed, next to Keegan, into a match-winning player. By the end of the season Newcastle had reached fifth position in the league, only missing out on promotion by three points. The supporters were disappointed but hopeful for the season ahead. Crucially, Keegan had committed himself to staying for at least another season at Newcastle.

In September 1983 Kevin Keegan was at Heathrow airport awaiting a flight up to Newcastle. A quiet figure who had come in on a different flight watched him carefully as he walked across the departure lounge. Too shy to approach the famous man, Peter Beardsley left it to Keegan to talk to him once they had landed in Newcastle. They took to each other from the start, which was apposite, because between them they were going to save the club.

The first irresistible sign that Newcastle were on to something came in a home game against Manchester City on October 29. Beardsley scoring a hat trick, Waddle a goal, and Keegan inspired the whole performance, even finding time to score a goal himself.

That season Keegan scored 27 goals, Beardsley 20 and Chris Waddle 18. It was due to playing with Keegan that both players realised their ability, and Beardsley, in particular, would never forget it.

After Keegan's last game, a home match against Brighton, was over and promotion in third place assured, Keegan left St James' Park and Newcastle by helicopter. He was to disappear from football for eight years of golf and business deals, flitting between Hampshire and the Costa del Sol.

'Playing at Newcastle was a marvellous experience and it matched any other I've had, I couldn't have ended it all in front of better people...it was a personal tribute to them.' It was a self indulgent way to pay Newcastle's supporters a compliment, but it got Keegan his headlines. Among the following pack of ball boys who watched in wonder as Keegan helicoptered away that night was one youth who had decided that he would become a professional footballer too. Alan Shearer was his name.

'The things that I was promised'

The obvious choice for the Newcastle manager's job in 1992 would have been Arthur Cox. Not only was he perfectly suited to the job but he had only left the position in 1984, after four years, because he felt that the club were not committed to buying players. Now, with Sir John Hall in place at the club and the talk of the money to be spent, Cox was popular with the supporters, the local press and with several members of the Newcastle board.

But sponsors have more influence than supporters, and the club's finances were still dependent on the attitude of amongst others the Newcastle Breweries, and the Newcastle Breweries wanted a name big enough to generate massive publicity. Hall, himself of a like mind, well understood the breweries' pressure on him to go for Keegan, as well as realising that if the club were relegated to the Third Division they might cease to exist at all. Hall as much as admitted that he had been given no choice in the matter only a few days after Keegan arrived as the new boss: 'If Kevin had not agreed to come back here as manager, our financial backers made it clear they would have to pull the rug from under our feet. We had to restore the confidence of these people or there would have been no Newcastle United. To put it simply, it was Keegan or bust. Even though Kevin Keegan has come back we are still on a knife-edge. I have to admit if it had been anyone else but him I wouldn't have gone along with it.'

Keegan had other backers as well. Hall's son Douglas was convinced that Keegan was the right man and he was supported in his opinion by chief executive Freddie Fletcher. So, ten years after he had come to the club as a player, Keegan found himself again involved in clandestine meetings in London hotels with the officials of Newcastle United. The deal was offered on Tuesday February 4,1992, in the Hilton Hotel, and that night when Keegan returned home to his wife she looked at him and said, 'You are going, aren't you?' He was.

The appointment was made public the next day, which was news to the man who thought he still was the manager of Newcastle United, Ossie Ardilles. Only recently given the dreaded 'full confidence' of the club, he was consequently a little surprised to find Freddie Fletcher on his doorstep at eight o'clock in the morning. Fletcher handed Ardilles an envelope which contained his reward for attempting to create an attractive and successful football team on Tyneside, the sack. Hall was brusque in his defence of the quick about-turn that he and the club had given Ardilles. 'This is our last attempt at survival. Confidence in the club, despite all the massive problems, is the key to our entire rescue strategy. I was still standing by Ossie Ardilles as manager even after we lost 5-2 at Oxford last Saturday, but the confidence of those who are part and parcel of the operation had collapsed.' So it was the financial institutions, the banks and the breweries who betrayed Ossie Ardilles, not Sir John Hall. Ardilles' response was eloquent in its simplicity, 'My heart is broken.'

Three hours after Ardilles' heart was broken a press conference was convened at St James' Park. It isn't often that the press is openly shocked, but this time the journalists were genuinely taken aback. In part this was due to the sheer theatrical indulgence of the show that was put on for them, but mainly it was down to the audacity of what Newcastle United were doing.

Sir John Hall, shiny headed and full of the importance of the occasion, appeared at the conference podium (podium appearances were going to become characteristic of Newcastle United over the next five years) and announced, 'Ossie Ardilles has left the club...' Before the full surprise could register on the assembled jowly faces, a curly-headed figure came into the room. Hall continued, '...and here is the new manager.' Kevin Keegan was back, there was no helicopter this time, but it was an entrance no less conspicuous than his earlier departure from St James' Park had been.

Keegan stated his intentions: 'Newcastle United have tremendous potential but that is only any good if you can realise it. But we have a major plus-point, the best fans in the country. These people will turn this club around, with help from us. I haven't signed anything as yet but everything is agreed. My contract will last as long as it is necessary to turn this cub around.' From his first utterance as manager Keegan was allying himself to the supporters and what he felt they deserved; if he was going to be a champion at Newcastle United he would be a peoples' champion.

'This was the one job I had to say yes to. I have turned them all down. I would not have gone to Liverpool, Southampton or any other club – just Newcastle United. Since retiring as a player I have had lots of offers from big clubs at home and abroad. But this is the only club I would consider managing. I have always followed this club intensely and I thought this was the right time to come into management. I have always said I didn't want to be a manager, but sometimes you have to stand up and be counted. I don't want to take on failure. I don't have to take it. I want to be a success. It's not a desperation move at all. I am going in with my eyes open.'

And above all, it was the fans that brought him back. Two years later Keegan looked back at what motivated him to return to Newcastle: 'I played for Liverpool against Newcastle in the 1974 Cup Final at Wembley. We hammered them. The Newcastle fans had every right to walk out, yet they sang. A lot of people remember that as the best cup final in terms of fans. There was part of me saying this is one club I played for that has never fulfilled its potential, not in my lifetime. The year I was born, 1951, Newcastle won the FA Cup. They won it again in 1952 and 1955, but in the league they have always threatened, never delivered.' Keegan could not have known then how ironic his words would ring five years later, when the only tangible reward for his messianic leadership would be an old First Division Championship and several seasons of coming close but not close enough.

Amidst the euphoria around the messiah's return the fact that

Keegan had never managed a football team before was forgotten. Although he was confident in his prediction that Keegan would succeed, it took Keegan's ex-manager at Newcastle, Arthur Cox, to give some note of relative calm to the proceedings. 'It's not for me to speculate on precisely why it was that Kevin stayed out of the game for so long. Obviously, he had his reasons but it's interesting to note that it took Newcastle to tempt him back. He had a special relationship with the people of the north-east during his time as a player at the club and it touched him deeply. I'm very proud of the fact that it was me who took him to Newcastle in the first place. It was me who persuaded him to join the club although, to be honest, he did not need much persuading. I simply told him that I needed him, the club needed him and the people needed him. I think Kevin will make an even bigger mark as a manager than as a player. Bearing in mind his achievements at Liverpool, Hamburg, Southampton and Newcastle United, that is quite a bold statement, but he's the sort of man who will succeed at anything once he has committed his heart and soul to the venture. This is the sleeping giant of football Keegan is trying to rouse. And he's the right man to do it. I'm now saying to Kevin what Bill Shankly said to me, "If you are successful with Newcastle, son, there's not a block of granite at Aberdeen big enough to build you a throne." Kevin has taken a lot of decisions in his career, and he has made them work. I know him. I know of his knowledge, his understanding of men, his enthusiasm and determination.'

However, Cox added, 'He'll have to sit and squirm like the rest of us. For once, his destiny is not in his own hands. The fans are already thinking he'll turn things around immediately. They believe he has the Midas touch. They expect him to do as a manager what he did as a player. He only had to look after himself before. He knew he could carry the team on his back. He can't do that sitting on the touchline. He was the finest example any young footballer could copy, because he wasn't blessed with everything. God didn't shine on him the way he shone on Johan Cruyff, Kenny Dalglish or George Best. Keegan made himself into a player by work, work, work. In a way, it made him intolerant of some other players at Newcastle. He disliked the thought of anyone being overweight. Kevin couldn't take it when he saw a kid who couldn't pass the ball. He believed that if you worked and practised hard enough you could overcome anything. He was intolerant of Chris Waddle at first. And, for six months, Waddle fell by the wayside. He could be the making of some of the youngsters at Newcastle now. But others might not survive him. Waddle bounced back but others died away. They couldn't handle the expectations and the 30,000 crowds. All that will happen again.'

Cox wasn't only mindful of the players who were bound to drop by the wayside if Keegan took hold of the club, he knew also it was dangerous to be disingenuous with Newcastle United and its supporters. It was no good mouthing platitudes about the re-birth of a great cub. It had to be done properly or not at all. Arthur Cox knew that Keegan hadn't come out of retirement to play at managing.

'He can turn Newcastle into the Glasgow Rangers of our game. They could dominate English football. The big "if" concerns his backing. We know how big Kevin Keegan is. We know the size of Newcastle's support. But how big are Sir John Hall and the directors? We are about to find out. They have to back him, otherwise the wrath of the people will pour down on them. If they push the boat out, wipe off the debts and help him buy class players then Newcastle can be mighty. You can look at that handsome face and charming smile and get the wrong impression. Underneath it all, he's a hard little so and so. I don't even consider the possibility he might fail. Not if the directors are worthy of him. If he is to build Newcastle into the kind of club the people up there deserve, then he's going to need the help of those who have given him the most demanding job in the game.' In reality that meant one man, Sir John Hall.

Shortly before Keegan arrived, the man who brought him to Newcastle had finally arrived himself. John Hall had been involved with the club for several years but only recently had he won his battle for control of the boardroom, and now in a position of authority he intended to revolutionise Newcastle United. Hall was man of the eighties; he had taken the soulless free enterprise message of the Thatcher government to heart and added a certain amount of Geordie charm to the Tory mantra of personal achievement. By the canny process of building retail space on the land that the Thatcher years had denuded of industry, Hall had made himself enough money to indulge in every working-class boy-made-good's dream, running his own football club. It was to be a strange, and ultimately untenable coupling for both men.

Hall was perceptive enough to know he needed someone who was already a hero to the Geordies, who had the respect of the players but who was also, and this was the most fundamental quality that Hall was looking for, a big enough name to attract players to Newcastle and to generate the publicity that Hall was desperate for. Almost alone amongst football chairmen at that point, Hall had worked out that publicity equals money. He also had a vision: 'I have this dream of a sporting club built around Newcastle United. I was very influenced when I travelled to Spain and Portugal and saw Barcelona, Real Madrid, Benfica and Sporting Lisbon. The old fascist governments built these stadiums before the war, so the clubs don't own them. The governments fund them and the clubs don't have to put all the money in as we've had to do.'

A typical Hall performance. An easy going discussion of the relative merits of fascist sports policy coupled with his one idea, if you want to do something, go and watch the people who do it best.

Hall's millions had come form the Metro centre, a massive shopping complex south of the Tyne in Gateshead. Inspired by the shopping malls he had encountered in the United States of America, Hall set out to convert derelict industrial land in the north-east into prime retail space. He now intended to apply that theory to running a football club. Hall's ambitions were beyond grandiose; within a few years he would compare Newcastle United to some of the biggest footballing institutions in the world.

'We're a one-club city. We've got a million people to draw upon. Barcelona have more because they are a semi-national state, the Catalans; while Real Madrid are traditionally the

Spanish club. We're a provincial club, but we have a loyal and fanatical following which gives us brand leadership and awareness. We have an influence way beyond the boundaries of St James' Park. Newcastle United only takes £12 million from the turnstiles and we need another £50 million to compete with the Barcelonas and the Real Madrids. If I don't get the business side right, we'll never be able to reinvest in our equity, which is the players. I'm the strategist and the dreamer, the one that looks at the global vision for Newcastle United. I'll tell you now a lot of changes are going to come. We've got history and tradition on our side, but we're not quite an institution in terms of having won things. We'll start to win things from now on. In the next few years we'll be winning the leagues and cups.'

As well as being an astute planner, Hall was an awe-struck millennial dreamer, and consequently every statement, every public announcement that he delivered would be laden with meaning. For Keegan it would be akin to having a mixture of John F Kennedy and T Dan Smith as his boss, and for Hall, as Keegan's employer, it would be no less testing.

The chairman was given an immediate demonstration of what he had unleashed. On February 8, 1992, Hall watched Keegan's new charges beat Bristol City 3-0 in his first match in charge. For the heart-broken Ardiles it must have been more than galling to see his team play with a certitude and self-confidence rarely demonstrated under his command. Keegan had already noted the bad morale amongst the players.

'The biggest problem I have here is to lift everyone. Not the fans; I don't know what keeps them going, but they seem to be immune from all the doom and gloom. I'm talking about the players, and everyone else behind the scenes. Little things can make a difference to morale, and the first thing I've done is clean up the training ground. It is going to be sold, so the club are not prepared to put money into it, and I can understand that, but it's going to be my home for the next thirteen weeks and home to my players too, so it should be kept decent. How can I tell my players that this is the best club in the world when the bath is not clean and the tiles are dirty? It's much nicer to come in and smell the disinfectant, and the first thing I've done is put that right.'

Toilets cleaned, messiah in place, there was only one more task to be completed before the ceremony could begin. Keegan needed an assistant. So with an eye to the stability that Liverpool had enjoyed over the previous 20 years it was a former Anfield and St James' Park colleague who Keegan called upon to join him – Terry McDermott.

'I have to have someone here who I know is completely on my side. Terry is my man. I haven't slept for two nights because I haven't had anyone to bounce anything off. Now I've got somebody who I know is completely on the same wavelength. Terry McDermott is very highly regarded in football, and he hasn't cost the club a penny. His money is coming out of my deal, so he's a real bonus. He'll help out on the coaching side, go and watch players, and generally lift the atmosphere through his personality. I can't ring up Arthur Cox. He works for Derby County. I can't ring my wife Jean because these are football things. The qualifications we've got are that we have known success, we were both winners. I think I can motivate, and I know Terry puts a smile on people's faces. To me we are far more qualified than some of the people who get the badges and have never been there. Terry will be my buffers. Terry is completely different to me, he was successful as a player without making it a life or death situation. I know Bill Shankly said football is more important than life or death, but Terry bucked the trend, and he's here now because I trust him and he's my man. He's not here in any particular capacity other than to add to the atmosphere of the club. I have to have someone to help me who is on my side and Terry fits the bill. My biggest problem is to lift people.'

Already personally enthralled by Keegan after their experience playing together, McDermott was the perfect choice as a go-between for Keegan and the playing squad. Though by no means stupid, McDermott cultivated a boyish humour that appealed to the adolescent ethos of football players. Although Keegan liked the occasional practical joke, McDermott was a man ill at ease with the serious, a school boy with a greying mop, his would be the grin that would cover for the anguished wince his boss would wear with such regularity over the coming years. Uncomfortable with personal attention and unassuming to the highest degree, in 1992 McDermott was happily retired from the game and had no thought of going back into football at all. But Keegan's invitation to join him was the one opportunity he could not turn down. McDermott said of his appointment, 'This will be a lot harder than our first time here when we were players. I am certain Kevin will turn this club around and I would love to be part of it and I will help Kevin in any way I can. I always remember Bob Paisley saying he was Shankly's buffer, well now I'm Kevin's buffer and I'm here to work hard. I never thought about coming back until I got the call from Kevin.'

References to Liverpool flying, Keegan remarked, 'This situation is very similar to the club that Shankly inherited. I want to carry it on because this club can be comparable to Liverpool.'

The Newcastle players were as captive as the rest of Tyneside in the excitement of Keegan's arrival, and played accordingly. Before the Bristol City game, on Strawberry Place, the road that runs alongside what was then the Gallowgate End of St James' Park, the queues of expectant supporters doubled in on themselves to accommodate a crowd that had increased from the usual 17,000 to nearly 30,000. Mounted policemen forced their way through the lines of supporters, but even the traditional enemy of the northern working-class, the law on a horse, couldn't raise tempers that day. The famous Strawberry pub, adjacent to the ground, was witness to the brand of inflated talk that only years of disappointment allied with a large lunch-time drink can produce. Keegan's apt description of Newcastle's record in the league, 'They have always threatened, never delivered,' was soon forgotten as the city's pubs gave in to the philosophy of 'just add beer for instant champions'. And that afternoon it seemed as if the drinkers from the Strawberry were right. The 3-0 victory was an appendix to the real matter of worshipping the returning hero, there was never a question of Newcastle failing to beat the 11 Bristol City players with walk-on parts. Virtually every chant that afternoon was addressed personally to Keegan, a collective love song that left the object of desire dizzy-headed and smitten. Keegan took in the adulation and gasped, 'I didn't know how the lads would respond to me at three o'clock, but I got the response I wanted. What I did know from my past experience here as a player was that the crowd would lift the team. The supporters were brilliant. It's not real out there. You just sit there and pretend you know what you are doing.'

He may have been pretending but Keegan was wise enough to know that one quick victory over Bristol City would not be enough. It's said often but it remains worth repeating that playing nice football isn't enough to get a team out of relegation trouble. Famously Nottingham Forest were relegated from the Premiership in 1994 under the tutelage of Brian Clough playing very good football; they were commonly held to be too good to go down. Likewise Keegan's predecessor Ossie Ardilles had kept his Newcastle side playing a typically pretty passing game that had seen them beaten week after week by second-rate sluggers and long-ball teams. That same season, before his appointment as manager, Keegan had attended Newcastle's home match against Blackburn Rovers. Partly through necessity and partly for the sheer pleasure of it, Ardilles had given youth its head at the club, and Keegan had been aghast at what he had seen, 'It was like watching a youth team. I was still in the Fourth Division at their age. You won't get out of the Second Division with just kids.'

Keegan would later go on to react against criticism of the cavalier approach of his later Newcastle sides by saying he would 'always play football the way it should be played', but in the dull winter of 1992 he knew survival would come down to a dour fight to the finish. Keegan knew he must spend some cash and at this point he was confident that Hall's promise of adequate funds to build a team would materialise, and he spoke with good-natured envy about Kenny Dalglish's position at Blackburn Rovers, where the steel magnate Jack Walker had presented his manager with an open cheque book. 'What would Newcastle give to be in a similar position? There were more than 23,000 for that game [Newcastle v Blackburn] and you would fill St James' Park if the manager was given the money to bring in the players he wanted.'

To that end Keegan invested almost immediately in two players who would give Newcastle depth and strength. Ironically, given his later reputation as a spendthrift, the first was a free transfer – Kevin Sheedy, who came to Newcastle from Everton. The Eire international had been a key player of the eighties midfield at Goodison, teaming-up with Paul Bracewell, Peter Reid and Trevor Steven to help the Merseysiders to a brace of championships. At Newcastle he secured the centre of the team and his vision opened up new opportunities for the forwards. Anchoring his defence Keegan opted for a man who looked more at home in a Norse myth than a football field, Brian Kilcline. A huge man, Kilcline arrived from Oldham Athletic for £400,000 with long yellow hair and the sort of moustache more commonly associated with the occupants of long boats. His presence alone was enough to deter any opposition attackers who had not been put off already by his nickname 'Killer'. Not a typical Keegan player, but an effective one.

The players were arriving at St James' Park, but for Keegan it was only a beginning. Combining the remains of Ardilles' youthful side with his recently acquired muscle and guile would not be enough to assure more than survival and even that was still uncertain. To achieve more than the minimum Keegan needed more players but he was no longer confident that he would get the cash to do this with. Promises are easily made and easily believed in the comforting atmosphere of the Hilton Hotel bar. In the real world at St James' Park it looked suspiciously to Keegan as if those promises were going to be welshed on. Arthur Cox's worries about Keegan being given the money he required to save Newcastle had become a pressing concern sooner than Cox could have imagined. Keegan saw personal betrayal in a situation which in truth was more a matter of confused finance than any real attempt to bamboozle the manager; the club was in a state of chaos with half the board at each other's throats over share dealing. Having told Hall how he felt about the situation Keegan reacted in the same way he always did when he felt he was being put upon. He walked out.

On the day before Saturday's home match against Swindon Town, Terry McDermott received an early lesson in just how unique an experience working with Kevin Keegan was going to be. Keegan put his assistant manager into a car, and instead of driving to the Maiden Castle training ground, headed for the hills. Surprised to be on the road out of the north-east instead of running the team through its training regime, McDermott contrived to persuade a still unsure Keegan to turn the car around and go back to Tyneside.

Before the game on Saturday morning the board met to discuss the much vaunted £13 million rescue package for the club, and worked out a formula to overcome their fiscal wrangling. Kevin Keegan came back to St James' Park and engineered a 3-1 victory over Swindon but, job done, he left again for his house in Hampshire, saying as he went, 'I feel I have not been given the things that I was promised.' Meanwhile, the board met again. Sunday was the expected day of feverish speculation; would Keegan come back? Did he mean it when he said he had had enough? The country was about to find that Kevin Keegan treated walking out on Newcastle United much as Norman Stanley Fletcher had treated doing porridge; it was an occupational hazard.

Keegan knew from the moment he walked out that he had Hall and the club at his mercy. So confident was he that he talked to the press before he had reached a settlement with Hall, coming out on to the steps of his New Forest home to chat with reporters. 'It may be a crisis for them but it's not a crisis for me. I've got a smashing family, I'm at home with them and I'm having a pleasurable Sunday walk. As far as I am concerned it's all down to Newcastle. I left them in no doubt how I felt last Friday.'

By Monday Hall had capitulated and Keegan had won. By a torturous arrangement of intertwined loans and property deals that involved both the future development of the ground, and using part of Hall's home, Wynyard Hall, as security, the chairman contrived to raise £4 million and was able to offer Keegan an immediate £500,000 for players with the promise of another £1 million to follow quickly.

'I'm under contract to Newcastle United until the end of the season and this I will do. What I'm not prepared to do is to commit myself beyond that until a financial plan, which I understand from the chairman was agreed in principle by all directors on Saturday night, has been formally ratified by all board members.'

Hall had been pushed to the very edge, the £500,000 he had produced for players didn't come from the coffers of the club, it was his own and his wife's money that he gave Keegan. 'We are committing funds to the club to buy players and I will discuss that with Kevin. We are totally supportive of Kevin. There is money to buy players now and he will get it. You have to understand that this club is still on the verge of bankruptcy but we are committed to the rescue package and hope everything will come together in the next two months. I am happy, otherwise I wouldn't be putting the sort of money into the club I am. I'm putting a hell of a lot in, and that shows just how committed I am. We have total agreement and a common accord. I'm certain we can give Kevin the assurances he needs to keep at the club well beyond the end of the season. There are no differences between Kevin and myself. I am happy to say that we are both in this together and fully committed to this club.'

Hall was very much in Keegan's pocket. And it was Hall's pocket that was going to take the strain. However, it was McDermott who captured the course of events most astutely: 'Kevin doesn't bear grudges. There wasn't money available, now there is. All Kevin asks is to be allowed to manage the club the way he wants to. If he is, he will make Newcastle great again. If not, he will walk away again.'

Popular memory sees Kevin Keegan as an almost effortless saviour; he had merely to arrive at St James' Park to ensure Newcastle's survival and there was no possibility of relegation once Keegan had become manager.

But that was not the case and there was a very real possibility of Newcastle floundering under Keegan's first command. The fact that Newcastle were not relegated that season was due to Keegan anchoring his team around the man-mountain Brian Kilcline.

None the less, in the run in to the end of the season Keegan's team embarked on a series of results so poor it nearly finished off any chance of survival they had. On March 31 Newcastle played away at Wolverhampton – they lost 6-2; on April 4 they were beaten by Tranmere Rovers 2-3 at St James' Park; on April 11 they travelled to Ipswich Town and lost 3-2; on April 18 Millwall came to Newcastle and won by a solitary goal; two days later Newcastle lost 4-1 at Derby County. Newcastle were pitched back into the lower regions, the hellish placements at the bottom of the ladder.

Five failures in a row were five too many for Keegan and his team; at the Derby County match both the players and the management team's discipline suffered. The referee was harangued by Keegan, and his players lost their heads after Kevin Brock was sent off for stopping a shot with his arm. Kevin Scott followed his teammate for a second bookable offence barely halfway through the first half, and Liam O'Brien sparked-off after having words, the nature of which remains shrouded but is presumed ungentlemanly, with the linesman. The match had not augured

well as the start had been delayed by a bomb scare, and Keegan
became so upset during the afternoon that he even had words
with Derby's manager and his own ex-boss and friend, Arthur
Cox. For Keegan to lose his temper with Cox indicated just how
adversely he was taking the fast-approaching and cavernous
prospect of falling into Division Three. Unwilling to articulate
male closeness beyond inverted paternalism, the immature
world of football is awash with surrogate father-son relationships, and Cox and Keegan fitted the cliché, Cox himself always
quick to give his support and praise to his ex-protégé, saying
once, 'Kevin epitomises everything you would want to see in a
young footballer. His attitude, his manner, his dedication were
all exemplary. He's a very special person.' A very special person
perhaps, but on this occasion Keegan's attitude and manner
failed to be exemplary. He didn't believe what was happening
to him and as Brain Kilcline put it, 'The boss was gob-smacked.'
Keegan followed referee Brian Coddington down the tunnel at
the end of the game, berating both him and his decisions. The
police were obliged to move in on the away end and calm down
the Newcastle supporters who were by now showing a little less
of their legendry good humour and were instead throwing seats
on to the playing field.

Keegan was no cooler after a post-match shower. 'You'd
better ask the referee what that was all about. He's the only one
who knows and he's still in there hiding. I've no idea why Terry
was told to leave the touchline. It seems to me referees have suddenly become the most important men in football.' Reasonably
enough Coddington reported the raging Keegan to the FA and

later in the year Keegan was fined £1000. This was small beer financially for Keegan, but that was not how he saw it: he wasn't being punished (hardly punished at all, given his income) he was being picked on.

'This was a one-on-one down the tunnel, I shouldn't have done it, but I just told the referee what I thought. I would have accepted it [FA disciplinary action] if it had been on the pitch in front of other people. But it was just me and him. A warning would have been acceptable and that's what I expected. This is over the top. I know what I did was wrong, but I don't deserve this punishment. They just thought, "It's Kevin Keegan!" I haven't stepped out of line often, but whenever it has happened I have been given the absolute maximum.' Keegan seemed less outraged about the £250 fine Terry McDermott received for his behaviour, 'Terry knows he got what he deserved.'

After Derby, Newcastle had two games left – at home to Portsmouth and away to Leicester City. Portsmouth were beaten 1-0 with a David Kelly goal. It was probably his most important goal of the season, perhaps of his career. But still Newcastle needed to win the last match, and the season came in the end to depend upon a trip to Leicester City. Keegan and McDermott had been brought in to save the club, but they were now faced with the horrible proposition of presiding over its demise as an important club in England. Keegan remembered when talking to Tyne Tees Television, 'It was a really strange feeling for me and Terry McDermott, we were coming to the end of our contract...in many ways we were in charge of our last game and I didn't want to be the manager who took Newcastle United down. In some ways it wasn't fair on us, we had inherited somebody else's players, we inherited a club that was absolutely devoid of leadership from the top to the bottom. We found ourselves in a boat trying to paddle out with people who I think, if we were honest, wouldn't have been our choice as players.' The team that wasn't completely Keegan's choice that day was Wright, Ranson, Neilson, O'Brien, Kilcline, Scott, Carr, Peacock, Kelly, Sheedy and Brock. Although they were a disparate collection of players who were to put Keegan through virtually the full range of emotions available to the human consciousness that afternoon, they were going to come through. With some unexpected help.

In the first half Newcastle set out with a studied determination to win, sadly this was not matched with the cool-headed accuracy the occasion demanded. Brock and Peacock both had opportunities which they hit over the Leicester crossbar, and the thought began to dawn that Newcastle were fated not to score. But then a different fate stepped in the shape of Leicester's Steve Thompson who, pressurised and disoriented, passed the ball into the path of Gavin Peacock. This time Peacock, showing all the composure and presence of mind that could be required, calmly scored.

1-0 up for much of the match, Keegan paced the line in a grey double-breasted jacket and dark slacks. His hands in his pocket and lips screwed tightly together, he was an essay in tenseness. Terry McDermott fluctuated between sitting on the bench in knee-crossed concentration and standing up to join his manager. When he did, McDermott shouted out the instructions, Keegan compressed his lips even further, so much so that they threatened to disappear into his mouth and down his throat. Keegan's hand came out of his pockets to clench air every time Newcastle came close to scoring again. If Keegan and McDermott thought this was heart stoppingly tight, it was going to get tighter. Leicester increasingly put more pressure on the Newcastle defence and within a few minutes of the end of normal time Newcastle broke. A long throw in from the left bounced around the heads of the Newcastle defenders who, characteristically, failed to clear it, and eventually the ball arrived at the head of Steve Walsh who directed it carefully outside of the reach of Wright. This surely was the end for Newcastle, the team's heads fell as one, sensing that there was no hope now. For the first time in their league history Newcastle were about to drop out of the top two divisions. The away bench became, for an instant, a place of despair. Keegan, one arm folded under the other, rubbed nervously at his mouth and nose. Suddenly he was dependent on the results of the other struggling Second Division sides, he looked up to the directors' box to see if his own directors had any intimation of what was happening elsewhere. Half the Newcastle bench looked angry, but McDermott and Keegan looked, instead, empty.

But this was a story that did not know its own limits; as Keegan looked at the immediate prospect of his time at the club ending in ignominious failure, the narrative of his journey with club was about to begin in earnest. The full 90 minutes had already passed by when Newcastle United's goalkeeper Wright punted the ball up field more in despair than in hope. It travelled high and it travelled long, so long that it bobbled just outside of the Leicester penalty area. As it bobbled Walsh, so recently the hero, attempted to pass it back to his own goalkeeper and what should have been an easy action transformed itself into a desperate stab at the ball with the end of his left foot causing it to travel inexorably into his own net.

For a moment Walsh stood transfixed, attempting to rationalise what he had just done. He had just saved Kevin Keegan and Newcastle United, and the few years of glory and near triumph that were to follow for Newcastle can all be traced back to that one unnecessary and scarcely believable toe-bung on a sunny afternoon in Leicester. Once the ball had rolled into the back of the netting the Leicester supporters invaded the pitch. There were a few minor fights, but for the most Newcastle's followers were too bemused or happy in the face of what they had just seen to get involved. The match ended a rather informal affair, chaos ensued after the pitch invasion and no one heard a whistle if one was blown. The Newcastle players ran to the sidelines and embraced the staff as Keegan shouted at them to get off the pitch. In the dressing room he told them that before they went on holiday they should be rightly proud of themselves for what they had done for Newcastle, though there is no record of him offering similar words of wisdom to Steve Walsh.

The Leicester City game had wrung out Keegan, McDermott and Hall. After the Leicester equaliser the manager and his assistant had taken on the appearance of haggard muppets, as if Bert and Ernie had suddenly been brought in by Hall to run the club.

Keegan and McDermott recovered, but from now on the club was going to experience its own puppet show and it would never be clear who was the puppet and who was the master. Both sides, Hall and Keegan, would have their hands on the strings, yet both sides would be made to dance. Meanwhile Newcastle United had, to quote one of the most apposite phrases in football, 'avoided the drop' and, like a man pardoned just as the executioner tightens the knot around his neck, Keegan intended to live a little. Only hours after the match he made clear to Hall what he would be expecting from the club. 'It's up to the chairman and the board to make sure we don't get into this position again. There is a meeting about the club's future on Wednesday and I have been told I'll know by May 11 whether I am to get what I want. If the directors come up with what I am seeking I'll be manager of Newcastle for the next three years. If they don't they'll have to find a miracle worker. I was promised money in February, it was needed then to turn things round and it still is. I want it now in writing. What I am saying to the board is, "Give me a chance to manage." If Newcastle don't want me I'll go back to my stud farm.' Whether his assertion that he should now walk away from the club for ever after kick-starting such a resurgence of hopes was heartfelt or merely disingenuous can perhaps be best gauged from the resulting scramble to keep him at the club.

'The last exciting piece of the jigsaw'

May 1992 was witness to next stage of the will-Keegan-go-or-will-Keegan-stay saga. The trigger to events was Sir John Hall finally achieving complete control of the club, increasing his personal share of Newcastle United to 64 per cent, and coupled with his son Douglas's shares, the Hall family had more than a 75 per cent stake in the club. Although Hall had initially wanted the club to be owned by supporter shareholders, events had forced him into a personal takeover; now that he was there Keegan expected him to provide the money to build a promotion-winning squad and as far as Keegan was concerned that meant at least £2 million for new players. In case his threats weren't being taken seriously, Keegan repeated his successful tactic of the autumn, he walked out, this time flying his family to Marbella. For once Hall lost his temper: 'I would like Kevin to remain here but it's no good him or anyone making unrealistic demands. This should be all about teamwork. How many other directors around the country have put in the sort of money that

I have pumped into the club? Since he has arrived Kevin has bought four players and that £600,000 has come out of the money Lady Hall and myself put in. In addition there is a £500,000 loan and more than £2 million from me through a shares issue. Lady Hall and myself have had enough in many ways. How much more have we got to put up with? I don't work willingly with a gun placed against my head, I never have. I have spoken many times about the club's financial position. If people are not prepared to take this into consideration, then so be it. We haven't gone down but the debts haven't suddenly gone away. I have kept quiet over the last few weeks. I didn't want to cause any problems. You see managers making demands, it's time directors started making demands. We only just scraped clear of relegation. You have to say, "What went wrong down below?"'

It was the first time that Hall had implicitly criticised Keegan's running of what Hall liked to call 'the football side of the club'. He had a point – Keegan was being lauded for an achievement that could be put down to luck as much as judgement.

Hall was now faced with the task of holding together a club that was still over £6 million in debt, dealing with a manager who perpetually pushed him to the edge, and the prospect of ex-chairman George Forbes replacing him at the head of the Newcastle board. Hall's initial attempts at a rescue package of the club, through his property company Cameron Hall Developments, which would have raised £13 million, collapsed. Hall nearly cracked, 'I don't need this hassle at my time of life. I am 60 next year and it's about time that I tended to the garden.'

Likely replacements for Keegan were being discussed openly

in England. The press's favourite choice, as it offered such a neat twist to the story, was that Keegan's former protégé at Newcastle, Chris Waddle, would return from French side Marseilles to take over at St James' Park. Searching for a solution that would save money and still keep the Newcastle supporters on his side, Hall saw Waddle as a cut-price Keegan, immensely experienced, a great playing record and popular with the supporters. But there were those at Newcastle who felt Keegan had to stay, and Hall knew as much himself. Within days of Keegan flying to Spain a club delegation followed him from Newcastle. Two directors, Hall's son Douglas and Freddie Shepherd, and chief executive Freddie Fletcher met Keegan, and in effect capitulated to him again. Keegan got his money for new players and a three-year contract for himself and McDermott. In the warmth of the Costa del Sol Keegan could afford to be magnanimous. 'My heart has always been with Newcastle and I always wanted to come back provided everything was all right. Now the uncertainty has been lifted and I'm ready to lift Newcastle to become a great club again. Things have been on hold for three weeks but that's not a disaster. I'll be moving my family up to the north-east now that my future is sorted out.' The depth of the rapprochement between the chairman and the manager became obvious when the public found out just where in the north-east Keegan was moving his family to: Sir John Hall's Wynyard Hall estate in County Durham.

Wynyard Hall was the former home of Lord Londonderry whose coal wealth had been earned on the backs of north-eastern colliery men; the irony that they were now living in the old boss's home wasn't lost on the two sons of pit men who were both representative of the new football money. Installed cheek by jowl with each other at work and at home, the two men's immediate futures were entwined. Keegan couldn't achieve anything without Hall, and Hall was by now personally dependent on Keegan staying at Newcastle. If Keegan went, Hall would be blamed by the supporters, and everyone else for that matter. All the traditional and deserved insecurity of the Tyneside public would be unleashed on the man who brought them a messiah only to lose him after three and a half months. How Hall felt about this situation can only be guessed at but in a few short months he had created his own Frankenstein. Hall had to keep Keegan, and Keegan knew it all too well.

Keegan cemented the renewed pact, 'We have been given a real chance to turn this club around and that is all we ever wanted. The chairman has given us a real chance to have a go. We have a lot of ideas to thrash out and the next two days are very important.'

Once it had been established that Keegan was staying at Newcastle United the club could embark upon the next leg of their journey – promotion to the Premiership. Realistically it would take time, or rather it would for any other club that had just marginally escaped relegation and whose players were a mixture of the past-it, the provisional and the possible. But Newcastle were different to any other team, and Keegan had unleashed something at Newcastle which would achieve its perfect expression in the 1992-93 season.

The summer saw Keegan embark upon a mass clear-out of players who were excess to his requirements. John Anderson went to Berwick Rangers, Darren Bradshaw to Peterborough United, John Gallacher to Hartlepool United, Lee Makel to Blackburn Rovers and David Robinson to Blackpool. Keegan took no joy in letting players go; he remembered only too well what it was like to be a young player himself. 'I was on £7.50 a week at Scunthorpe when I was an apprentice and I could live on that. My digs were £3.50 a week so I had to pay that and live quite comfortably on that. One of the lads even managed to buy a car, I don't know how much it cost him. The first-year apprentices were on £4 so in your second year you went from £4 to £7.50, which was a massive jump. But even the lads on £4 managed and we still had time to go down the town centre to play pinball machines and have the odd night out at a disco, be Jack the Lad, buy a few clothes as well. I don't begrudge my players a penny. If they come in to renegotiate a contract it's usually because I want them to stay. If I want them to stay it's because they have done well and if they have done well I want to reward them. I certainly get the young lads in very quickly if they have done well and up-grade them, I don't like young lads in the first team as cheap labour. I always give them a big appearance so that when they actually force their way into the first team and keep out an experienced player who's on a fairly good contract I make sure that they are rewarded for that, and of course theirs is a reward for success. You can't reward failure and some young lads come in wanting new contracts, and you just tell them the truth, they haven't done enough to deserve one and therefore maybe they should look for another club. And that's difficult because maybe you really like the lad and you know his parents or you've got to know his parents, that's difficult. That's one of the hardest parts, telling a YTS, "Thanks, we've enjoyed having you for two years but you're not up to the standard required to get a full-time contract." That's difficult for them and for me.'

As the unwanted went, the players who would make the season arrived. Paul Bracewell from Sunderland, John Beresford from Portsmouth and Barry Venison from Liverpool. Bracewell had just reached the FA Cup final with Sunderland, and that Keegan was able to bring him to St James' Park was an indication not only of the tremendous personal appeal he had himself to professional footballers but also the growing belief that if anyone could take Newcastle to the Premiership then Keegan could. Barry Venison agreed, 'The potential here is obvious. But speaking to Kevin and Terry McDermott convinces me that we are capable of achieving something this season, and by that I mean Premier League status.'

Keegan was buying the sort of players who could take the weight of a promotion campaign on their backs. 'Now, besides Killer (Kilkline) I have bought Barry Venison and John Beresford who are leaders, and Paul Bracewell who although he is injured I can't wait to have back. Suddenly you find all the others become leaders as well.'

Kilkline, such an important architect of the successful survival struggle, found himself side-lined already. Keegan wasn't going to let emotion or gratitude get in the way of what he wanted and who he would pick for the side. Kilkline did, at least, have the comfort of knowing he would be told bad news directly by Keegan, a fact Keegan was proud of. 'I learned a lot in terms of management from Lawrie McMenemy, especially that good players are always the easiest to handle. I think I'm still the kind of person I always was. I'm very honest with players. I would always tell them if a club had been in for them or that I was leaving them out of the side before they read about it in the papers.' His mentor, Shankly, used to ignore players he would not pick as for him they no longer existed; for Keegan they were to be treated honestly and fairly as long as they didn't cross him publicly. Constantly looking to build his list of players, Keegan added to his roster in September by buying Robert Lee for £700,000 from Charlton Athletic; it was to be one of the most astute uses of Hall's money that Keegan would make.

If there were any concerns about the fervour for football and Keegan continuing on Tyneside they were misplaced. The first game of the season, at home to Southend United, attracted a crowd of 28,545 – the biggest in England that day. The season started with an incredible run of straight wins in the first eleven matches. Southend United, Derby County, West Ham, Luton Town, Bristol Rovers, Portsmouth, Bristol City, Peterborough United, Brentford, Tranmere Rovers and Sunderland were all beaten. Newcastle were doing what was thought to be impossible, passing their way out of the First Division, and Keegan took pride in the fact.'We did it before in 1984 at Newcastle, but we only scraped third place. But I think football is changing and I'll tell you why it is changing. A lot of forwards are coming into management. You look at our league, Brian Little, Glenn Hoddle, myself. We are all forwards who wouldn't really know enough about to defending to coach it even, so maybe the trend is changing and maybe that is good for football. Maybe all the defenders who have had jobs in football, now they are going to be in a minority and forwards are going to have their day. That's not a bad thing. I just hope and pray that when we are live on television that we get a chance to show people what we have been doing. There is always the danger that you will have an off day, or that the other team, for whatever reason, dominate you, it can happen. But we've played some terrific football like you haven't seen in the Premier League so far this season. We've probably been playing the sort of football that you would have expected Nottingham Forest to have been playing. I think you can get out of the First Division by playing football now and I think the long-ball game is OK in the short term but there is no long life in it. Just look at Cambridge, the manager has turned round and said we are going to play a different way.

'Our fans are telling us that they like what we are doing and some of the other clubs who are having a bit of success but who are still not getting the crowds have got to say, "Hold on, here is the product that we are putting on the table but what do the fans want?" That's what you are governed by, the number of people who come through the turnstiles; if we lose sight of that then it will be a sad day for football. Playing in front of empty stadiums but with a good TV contract for me will not be a great setting to bring players on in. Sky do a terrific job but they oversell; I mean you're theirs two hours before the game, hyping the game up to be something it could never live up to, and has no chance of doing so from the minute the ball is kicked off. That will change, they'll realise that the fireworks at the end are worth nothing if there are no fireworks on the field. Dancing girls and singing are nothing if the game is no good. That is why 29,000 people are turning up at

A small man made big: Keegan's success at Liverpool was a triumph of will over skill

At Hamburg Keegan was twice voted European Footballer of the Year,
but he was at times a lonely and unpopular figure

An unruly international?
Pugnacious and confident
in his abilities, Keegan was
never far from controversy
in his England career

Swan song at St James' – Keegan's last season as a footballer saw Newcastle United promoted and the man become a messiah to the Toon fans

The second coming – Keegan's first game as manager.
Newcastle followed the script and beat Bristol City 3-0

McDermott and his manager: 'If Kevin asked me to go to Timbuctoo, I would try and find it for him'

After only his first full season at Newcastle, Keegan wins the First Division Championship

1993/4 season: Keegan's great achievement, taking his
newly promoted side to third place in the Premiership

One night at Anfield, the season all but ends in the final seconds

1995/6 season: The football is beautiful, but Keegan
must watch another game slip from his grasp

Newcastle only draw with Spurs and as expected come
second to Manchester United. Keegan salutes his still loyal flock

Keegan and Ferguson together for Euro '96. The picture
was faked and on Tyneside Ferguson's image defaced

Keegan sees Newcastle submit completely
to Manchester United in the Charity Shield

The joy of management. At times Keegan contrived to
appear powerless, surprised and weary all at the same time

Newcastle now, not because I am there, not because we've got Kevin Sheedy and Barry Venison and John Beresford. It's because we're putting something on the pitch that they want to see and they're now being locked out from seeing it. You can't hype that up. Hype will only take you so far, you have then got to stand up and be counted and the lads at Newcastle United have done that this season. We're bucking all the trends and it's nice that Newcastle should have that, it's a big club and it should have it. We are the leading club in the country in terms of being unbeaten and that's lovely for the supporters because they have had a lot of lean years where they have supported the club through thin and thin where there's been no thick, and that's good.'

Newcastle were playing with a confidence and verve that proved too much for their opponents, in particular Gavin Peacock was providing the dividend on Newcastle's investment on a new contract for a player who had attracted the attention of many Premier clubs. Keegan had moved Peacock forward and he revelled in the change, scoring five goals in the eleven victories. During the run Newcastle knocked Middlesbrough out of the Coca-Cola Cup, a double delight for Keegan and the supporters, the elimination of a Premiership team and an ancient enemy.

Four games into the run any supporters still worried that Keegan may disappear at any moment would have been relieved to discover that he was investing £10,000 in a private box at St James' Park so his family and friends could watch matches in comfort, proclaiming, with typical understatement, 'Once you get it started here, once you get it turned round, I, you, not even the most fervent supporter can know what could happen. It will be the biggest explosion of feeling football has ever known. Now I am involved the only thing that matters is this club and its future success. Everything else apart from my family comes way behind. I keep saying to my wife Jean it won't always be as hectic as this but fortunately for me she and the kids are football people. They all love the game.'

It seemed implausible that only a few months previously Keegan had been talking of his job having been done; a new contract had been signed and Keegan was once more talking as an agent for Sir John Hall's dream machine, asking north-eastern journalist Doug Weatherall, 'Why shouldn't we do a Leeds? It needn't take three years to turn a team round. I've signed three new players and that's a big proportion of a team. And we're on the lookout for the last exciting piece of the jigsaw. I'm happy to set myself the challenge. I'm not scared to be so optimistic, it would be wrong to have a negative attitude. I didn't convince Barry Venison to reject another Liverpool contract by telling him it would take three years to turn the club around. I didn't get Gavin Peacock to stay with us and turn down the Premier League by saying it'll take a long time. I'm able to tell the players they can play a big part in the club's history.'

If Keegan was looking for a place in the history books he was also aware that it would be more than a matter of football that would get him a page, Hall's job would be just as important. 'Our club is still in debt, but we are looking to speculate. The chairman has been a tremendous help. He has provided money to strengthen the team and the club and I am happy to accept the responsibility for results. That first crowd brought receipts of around £150,000. If we keep getting that sort of money it's great to know it will go into the club. And the chairman says 50 per cent of our lottery money will go on players.'

Yet again Keegan was going out of his way to praise Hall's contribution to the club, which after bullying Hall into doing what he wanted was the least that Keegan could do. But there was a deliberate reasoning to Keegan's free way with a compliment when it came to his chairman; through the simple device of praising Hall he made sure any long-term financial commitments Hall had given him were public knowledge in essence if not in detail. Continually thanking Hall for the money he put up for players was a near perfect way of making sure Hall kept supplying Keegan with cash. More than most managers this was vital for Keegan, for he was not a boss who would build up a side over the years by developing the young players; quite the opposite in fact as he would go on to disband the reserve side a few seasons later. Long-term production of players through development and coaching was not his objective, mainly because he knew it wasn't his main strength. Literally and figuratively Keegan was a good judge of horse flesh – if he was to win anything or build a great side it would be by buying the right players and that would need money.

This put Keegan in a strong situation. If Newcastle were to fail, blame might well be deflected on to Hall for not letting Keegan buy the players he wanted. It would be a trap that Hall could not escape from until Keegan himself escaped from the pressures of management. It was also a theory that was dependent on Keegan blending the right players; in the early part of the 1992/93 season that seemed to be happening and Keegan saw no reason for it not to go on. 'Well it's a record-breaking start to the season for the club. We've won eight on the trot and we won the last two games last season so that's ten on the trot in the league. People say it can't last for ever, but why not? AC Milan are still going strong and they don't have any God-given right to be the only team ever to go a lot of games unbeaten.

'I've got a very good side in our division; with the players we've got we have a class side. Now the things that can do you are complacency and over-confidence, and it's my job as manager to make sure that doesn't happen.But I want the players to be confident, I want the players to realise how well they are playing, I want the players to understand that there is no reason that it has to end. I think they are starting to realise it now. Why does it have to end at Bradford on Sunday or Tranmere at home next week? Why can't we win that game as well? All right, we know somewhere along the line someone is going to turn us over. I just hope when they do it is because they have played better than we have, and we've given our all and it has been a great game of football and we say, "Fair play to them, we've had a great start to the season and we have beaten a lot of teams, they deserved to beat us." In a perfect world that is how I would like it to end. I suppose in a really perfect world I don't want it to end and I don't think the players do. They realise that what I have been saying to them is true, it is not just hype, they are a different class to anything in this table when we play and if we match them for effort then our football will be the difference. We have got a lot of football for a First Division side and I haven't seen anybody yet who can get within a touch of us as a footballing team. There are other teams that are very fit, there are other teams that work tremendously hard, and that is a great credit to their managers, but as a footballing side we're in a league of our own at the moment, along with probably Glenn Hoddle's Swindon. They are the nearest to us.'

Keegan was a man who swung between commitments, deep down always ready to turn away. Conscious perhaps of his growing reputation not just as a successful manager but as a man who could not be completely trusted to finish a job he stated his commitment plainly, 'Whatever happens here I will never be in charge of another club. I'm committed here for three years but we've already started to think about things that could carry that on for a lot longer. We've had a good start but that's nothing if we don't build on it. The danger is in getting carried away and thinking that it's going to be a doddle season. It won't be.'

Although it would be an easier season than the supporters of Newcastle could have realistically hoped for, there was immediate disappointment to deal with when the running streak came to an end when Newcastle were beaten 1-0 by Grimsby Town. Keegan knew that the run had to end eventually. 'I told the players we would get beaten sometime but it didn't have to be this week. They had a chance of going into history.' Newcastle had failed narrowly to set a league record and morale was affected enough for them to lose their next match away to Leicester City; but after going to Birmingham and winning and then drawing at home to Swindon Town, Newcastle embarked upon another run, beating Charlton, Watford, Cambridge and Notts County. Gavin Peacock scored in every match and got two in the defeat of Swindon.

By now the nation was watching Newcastle with delight. It

was not just the quality of the football that was being enjoyed, the whole aura around Newcastle made copy that escaped the sports pages and reached the front of the newspapers. Hall and Keegan talked with such certainty about the limitless achievement that was open to the club, the city and the region, that no one saw fit to doubt them. Magazine articles were based around Keegan and his home at Wynyard Hall, sloaney rookie reporters were despatched from metropolitan lifestyle sections to investigate this mystery city, their only research being two hours watching *Auf Weidersien Pet* videos and a tentative sip at a bottle of Newcastle Brown Ale in a Kensington pub. When they got to St James' they were charmed senseless by the obsessional behaviour of Newcastle United's supporters.

St James' Park had become a cauldron of noise for home matches. Keegan well knew the effect this could have on visiting teams, seeing it as an asset that his team should capitalise on, the fact that they had the most intimidating ground in the division also meant that anyone could be beaten. Visually it was equally intimidating, row after row of black and white replica shirts had a startling power which one opposing manager had likened to 30,000 baying zebras. Newcastle's support had always been loud and numerous, but the increased amount of matches on television meant that the Toon Army were suddenly possessed of a reputation and collective personality whose effect was breaking out of the north-east and into the rest of the country. As football increasingly became a game that could be guiltlessly enjoyed by the middle classes as well as its bedrock support, the new television viewers in the south found that instead of being horrified by the barbarians from the north, they were attracted to them.

The more popular the supporters became nationally the more their fame antagonised the supporters of Manchester United who were used to being judged as the most numerous and forceful support in the north. The fact that many of them weren't in the north at all served to add to their insecurity when confronted by a Newcastle support that was unmistakably and overwhelmingly from the same city as the club. The consequent insecurity and bitterness in the ranks of Manchester United's following would lead to a bad feeling between the two sets of supporters that would colour the rivalry between the sides and later add even more to the personal pressure Keegan was put under to beat Alex Ferguson's side.

The more immediate effect of the rise of the Toon Army on Keegan was a reinforcement of the public perception of him as a man beholden to his personal following, and it was a perception that was largely correct. Where Keegan went the Toon Army followed, the cult of the personality he had unleashed when he first became a favourite of the Gallowgate had now grown into a monster that, if he wasn't careful, would devour him.

There were no such concerns amidst the mass psychology of the terraces. If there was talk of the Geordies becoming northern Uncle Toms, putting on a show for the metropolitan media to patronise, it wasn't heard on Tyneside, not yet anyway. Their love of the football Newcastle were playing was such an honest and beautiful thing that they couldn't have held their exuberance in check if they had been ordered to at gunpoint. Keegan understood them, 'When they see the quality of the football we are playing now it's like a drug to them, they can't get enough of it. You've got to remember these fans have driven down motorways and watched some really abysmal sides in Newcastle shirts. They ain't going to stop now they've got a side like this, and I don't blame them.'

The supporters were tasting success for the first time in many years, and with each victory and further move toward promotion Kevin Keegan was elevated even further in their affections. In turn this further enmeshed Keegan in a way that no manager had been obliged to contend with since Bill Shankly had basked in the red glow of Scouse adulation at Anfield. Shankly had revelled in the adulation, but even he had admitted that it could become a bind, saying, 'You never get away from it, you take it home with you, it's with you 24 hours a day.' Shankly had operated in a time when a manager went home after training for his tea; he was not obliged to give five interviews after every match, open supermarkets or negotiate product endorsements. Keegan was under a new kind of pressure, part businessman, part coach, part public relations representative and full-time messiah. It was a matter of course that somewhere in his dealings he would give in to that pressure, eventually.

Tyneside was so enthralled that the undeveloped St James' Park was unable to accommodate all those who wanted to come and watch. The disenfranchised, rather than tearing the gates down, had to content themselves with watching matches on television and going to the Maiden Castle training ground to watch the team and Keegan work out. Inside the training ground Keegan applied a philosophy that seemed to owe more to Sir John Hall's dreams of a centre for sporting excellence than any traditional notions on how to coach and train a football team. An exercise physiotherapist who had previously specialised in boxers was given the task of improving fitness, the goalkeeping coach was Jim Montgomery, who had become a Sunderland legend for keeping out Leeds United in the 1973 FA Cup final, and the running coach was the same woman used by the tennis player Jo Durie. Keegan went out of his way to let the supporters have unprecedented access to the team. No autograph hunter went unrewarded and no young supporter was snubbed. There were few other sides in the country that would have open training in the week of a big match. If other teams were sneaking silent watchers into the crowds of Geordies it wasn't doing them much good. Newcastle kept on wining regardless of who watched them working out their moves beforehand.

Not everyone was happy though. Although he had been Newcastle's top scorer over the previous two seasons and had been popular with the Newcastle supporters, the well-built striker Mick Quinn had suffered from injury and never really fitted in with Keegan's ideal of a quick-witted Newcastle attack that featured players of the calibre of Peacock and David Kelly who had scored 11 goals in the campaign to stay up. Not a man to take rejection lightly, Quinn had publicly labelled life at Newcastle under Keegan as 'a shambles'. By December he had been sold to Coventry City. A month later Quinn went public with just what he thought about Keegan. Ironically for a manager who prided himself on being fair by his players, it was his alleged lack of honesty as a manager that Quinn claimed to be enraged by. 'What really brassed me off about Keegan was that he was never man enough to look me in the eye and say that he didn't fancy me as a player. I started the season thinking I'd patched things up after being told to play for my place. That's hypocrisy for you.'

It was the worst possible challenge to Keegan, a public challenge that questioned his honesty and character and he reacted in kind. 'There used to be only one Judas, but there are now a number of them, all after their 30 pieces of silver. He's just another Judas to me and that's the finish of it. There is no way Quinn can slag us of after what we did for him. I even sent him a telegram before his first game for Coventry wishing him all the best. Now I hope he feels really good. Obviously players get disappointed. But I admire the ones who just take it on the chin.' That then was what happened to players that Keegan didn't fancy.

By December 1992, and uniquely for a manager who had only recently been flirting with Third Division football, the first serious talk of Keegan being given the England manager's job began. Tantalisingly Keegan responded to the speculation by saying, 'I wouldn't leave Newcastle for any other club job.'

After all he had done to keep Keegan, even when he wasn't sure whether it was the best option for Newcastle, Hall was now confronted with the prospect of losing him to the national side. Hall reacted by offering the prospect of more money and long-term security for Keegan. 'Kevin has surprised me. I'm a businessman and I knew how marketable he was. But what he and Terry McDermott have achieved is a miracle. We must get up this season and I believe we will. It's all that matters. The second we are up I will offer Kevin a new five-year contract but the plan we have here embraces the next five years and its success depends upon continuity. I am expecting Newcastle to get into the Premier League, with Kevin at the helm for a long time to come.' Hall may have been a businessman but he had seen over £6 million spent so far. 'Kevin has spent the money well and there will be more when he needs it. But I am no Jack Walker, it is my pension money I am spending but I'm prepared to speculate to accumulate.'

January ended with Newcastle ten points clear of second placed West Ham. As Keegan approached the anniversary of him and Terry McDermott being in charge at St James' Park it could be judged by most calculations to have been a successful year. Keegan looked to McDermott's part in the success. 'I knew I would need a friend, someone I could trust implicitly, someone who would not let me down. Terry has done everything I expected of him and much more. I know a few eyebrows were raised when he joined me. He had a reputation for being a bit of a Jack the Lad type, but I knew my man. There has been a lot done in the year since we came here and a lot of it could not have been done without him. He has been a revelation, even to me. The place was full of doom and gloom. Now everybody smiles. It is a happy place in which to work.'

Promotion was now well within sight and Keegan was talking of where Newcastle would be when he celebrated his second anniversary at the club. 'This time next year we'll be up there with the élite. We must get into the Premier League and then keep the momentum going. You must not go in there and get cold feet. We don't want to be silly and just talk about staying and consolidation. I believe that this club with its leadership on and off the pitch should be going in there to try and do what Leeds have done. They entered the big-time looking to be winners and that's right. From what I have seen of the Premier League we are not far from being able to achieve the same thing.'

Even Kenny Dalglish came out of his brooding silence to praise what Keegan was doing. 'Kevin came in last season to save Newcastle from relegation and he achieved that. Now this year they have been at the top of the table throughout. Obviously Kevin must have enjoyed his time at Newcastle when he was a player, he must have had a tremendous affection for the club and the people. And having returned as manager he has done tremendously well. He took Terry McDermott back with him and he has clearly been a great help to Kevin. And if they get promotion, Newcastle will add a tremendous amount to the league.'

In the next two months Keegan was spurring the team on with more buys. For a while Keegan had been conscious of a left-sided midfielder in Cyprus. Keegan seemed to rise personally to the challenge of over-coming complicated transfer dealings, and the Nicky Papavasiliou transfer was as complicated as his name. But once Keegan wanted a player it became a case of him against the world in order to get the man.

Although he only cost £125,000, getting him to Tyneside involved Papavasiliou, a Cypriot, making seven trips to Athens in order to get Greek citizenship. But as Keegan said, 'He's a little gem.' If the Cypriot was a gem, Andy Cole was to prove to be a gold mine.

When Keegan signed the centre forward Andy Cole in March he had found his 'last exciting piece of the jigsaw'. When he chose Cole the player was largely unheard of. Sir John Hall must have blanched at paying £1.75 million for a player whose only achievements to date were a turning out for the England U-21s and when playing for Arsenal he had been loaned out to Fulham and Bristol City. But although he joined the club late in the campaign, by the end of the season he would have scored 12 goals and assured success for Newcastle.

Cole's time at the club was in the most to be marked by an arrogantly taken pleasure in scoring goals. As a player he seemed immune to doubt in his own abilities, an illusion that would make it all the harder for Keegan to spot the personal difficulties that would mark Cole's career. The perfect Cole goal would result from a collection of accurate and imaginative passes that would see Newcastle surge forward from defence and end with Cole galloping into the goal mouth pointing with his outstretched finger to the exact point where he expected the ball to be delivered. And unfortunately for opposition goalkeepers that was exactly where it usually went, whereupon Cole would score with a curled-lip swagger.

In some ways this was Kevin Keegan's least complicated season at Newcastle United; things happened as he wanted them to, his abstract ideas became black and white actuality. But nonetheless success bred its own pressures and Newcastle matches were increasingly picked to be broadcast as the Sunday afternoon television game. Keegan, the family man, reflected upon it. 'I'm not sure it's good because you lose your family day. I'll give the players Monday off this week but then all their kids will be back at school. So there is good and bad, pluses and minuses, I'm not a great fan of Sunday football, there will be a limit to how many times we'll be on and I think that is fair. It would be a shame if we were picked nearly every week and that would mean us playing Sundays and not Saturdays. That can't be allowed to happen, we shouldn't be penalised and our families shouldn't be penalised because we have had a good start to the season. I think in the contract it's a maximum of four games which I think is plenty.' And, as ever Keegan put the interests of the supporters at the centre of his concerns, 'They've got families as well, not all supporters are 18 or 19 and free and easy. Some of our really good supporters are married with kids and they actually take the kids, but they are going to suffer as well on the Sunday. Also things like trains aren't the same on a Sunday. I don't care what British Rail say, you go from London to Newcastle and end up going through Birmingham because they do all the repairs on a Sunday. The roads are quieter, that's one thing, but Sunday night when you're driving back from a London game that's the worse night of the week on the motorways. So there are a lot of things that the League and TV have to consider before they say, "Yeah, that suits us." '

Sunday matches or not, by May Newcastle were virtually Champions. The game against Oxford United on the May 6 was an opportunity for Newcastle to celebrate. And they did by winning 2-1.

There was much talk was of the extent of the club's achievement, and Terry McDermott was happy to explain how Keegan had personally enervated the side. 'He is so infectious. Even in training you might come in a bit lethargic. Then he comes in. He's bubbly and makes you feel better straightaway. This applies to his own training. The players look at him bouncing around at 42 years of age. Lads of 25 look on thinking, "Well, we had better do that." For the first time in the 20 years I have known this club I feel that we are heading in the right direction. We have the right person at the helm in the chairman, and a manager who is as positive as you can possibly be. There will be new players coming in. Everything augurs well for the future. They say you can't change a club in a year, it's supposed to be impossible. Well, they have done it here.'

Once more Keegan looked beyond the what Newcastle were doing to what he hoped they would do, once again comparing his side to Howard Wilkinson's Leeds team, 'We are looking to do what Leeds United did. They won the League in their second season back. There's no reason why we can't emulate that.' He also found time to send Sir John, who had been publicly discussing a new contract for Keegan and McDermott, a coded message. 'I've a good two-year contract. This is my club and if I leave it will be for something unforeseen.' At Newcastle the bargaining and shuffling for position never stopped.

The Championship was decided with an evening victory at Grimsby. Cole started it and Kelly finished it; having won 2-0 the last match of the season was immaterial. Like the year before it was against Leicester City but this time round the atmosphere could not have been more different. A year before Newcastle had been desperate to win, the pre-match talk was of how the other teams in relegation trouble would do and whether Newcastle had the grit to see them through. The pre-match talk this time was of how to arrange a party. The plans for celebration got so out of hand that Keegan had to step in and insist that there were no dancing girls on the pitch before the match. He wanted the razzmatazz to be during the match and he wanted Newcastle to gain as many points as possible from the season; nothing should detract from the football team and what it could do. He didn't see the match as a party but as an opportunity to give the Premier League a demonstration of exactly what Newcastle was capable of. He wanted a serious match and he wanted the season finished off in style. The team that took the field was very different to that which had gone out against Leicester 12 months previously; in place of a piecemeal side there was a finely crafted footballing unit: Srinicek, Venison, Beresford, Robinson, Scott, Howey, Lee, Cole, Kelly, Clark and Sellers. Before they could start the game the team indulged in the one piece of showmanship which couldn't be denied them or the supporters. One by one they lifted the Championship trophy to the crowd.

Some teams are arrogant in their pomp, but Keegan's side took an impish pleasure in what they were doing, they did not set out to crush Leicester but to dazzle them. The flow of Newcastle's game represented everything that Keegan wanted from a football team. If the previous season had been grim, this was delightful; every player moved off the ball offering options to his colleagues that continuously baffled Leicester, passes were accurate and usually one touch. As the sun shined down on St James' Park those present witnessed a display of football that produced seven goals from Newcastle, so complete was the overawing of Leicester that when they did score a final consolation goal to bring the score to 7-1 the Newcastle crowd applauded in sympathy.

At the end of the season Newcastle were eight points clear of the nearest contenders West Ham. They were the champions of the First Division, and easy champions at that, but Keegan was already looking to the next season: 'Tell Alex Ferguson we're on our way.'

'This is my England'

In the summer of 1993 there was again talk of Keegan leaving Newcastle and once more Sir John Hall was blanching at the prospect of another large buy. But the player Keegan was to sign in July would turn out to be worth all the £1.5 million Newcastle spent on him. Keegan wanted to bring Peter Beardsley back to his native city, but for John Hall it looked suspiciously like bad business to spend all that money on a player who appeared to be approaching the end of his career at Everton. Keegan however was adamant and Hall did what he usually did when confronted by Keegan, he relented. Beardsley was signed. Keegan knew he had won a vital battle. 'Peter was a very important signing, we were always an exciting side but throw him in and anything could happen. It's a case of lighting the blue touchpaper and standing back. You could write a book on what he might do for us, he can bring on young players like Clarke and Cole for a start, but we're going back into the big league and Peter, in one word, gives us credibility.' Hall would later admit that he has been mistaken, 'I thought Peter Beardsley was too old and Kevin said, "No he's not," and he has proven me wrong.'

Keegan knew he needed a player who was experienced at playing at the very top of English football, and once he had got him he could afford to be magnanimous. 'I like Sir John's openness and I think Terry and I are also open on our side of it. The chairman and I are quite different types of people, but his principles are sound, and we have a strong partnership. He's never, not even once, said to me, "You're not getting the money to buy that player." He's debated and argued about signings. Peter Beardsley was one in particular he really didn't want to have. That was partly my own fault, because when I signed Andy Cole and Robert Lee I was stressing they were the right age. If Cole hadn't made it with us, I knew that we'd get our money back-plus on Andy when he was 25, because he had pace and he would still be young. Peter was over 30, and I had to explain to the chairman that sometimes a gem pops up who can bring you qualities all the others can't. When that happens you've got to take the chance. Sir John opposed the signing on the grounds that it was a lot to pay for a 32-year-old. His point was a sensible one, but he's been the first to admit that we got it right. When we bought Beardsley we bought ourselves credibility in the Premiership. When Terry and I looked at the squad we had, we knew that Lee was a good player, but he'd only made a couple of dozen appearances in the Premier League. Scott Sellars hadn't quite made it, Barry Venison had been at Liverpool but wasn't really a regular. We were short on experience, but after buying Peter you could step back and say, "That's a real good side." '

It was all the more galling for Keegan then that Beardsley was forced to miss the start of the season after injuring his cheek in a pre-season friendly and was not able to make his début until the 2-2 draw with Swindon on September 18.

Premiership football immediately proved to be a much tougher proposition than winning the First Division. Newcastle lost their first two matches 1-0 to Tottenham and 2-1 to Coventry City. From the first 12 matches Newcastle contrived to win on only four occasions. But a spell of four matches from October 30 onwards saw Newcastle beat Wimbledon, Oldham Athletic, Liverpool and Sheffield United.

Considering what Keegan had done so far he could have been excused for sitting back to a degree, letting himself relax in the warmth of what had been achieved, slipping off the shroud of pressure that had been enveloping him. Instead he pushed himself even harder. When Keegan said he thought Newcastle could be Champions he meant it, and his ambitions on the football field were of the same order as Sir John Hall's were off it. And why not? What Keegan had done so far was remarkable, surely he could do even more. Yet to keep up the campaign Keegan was obliged to push himself even further personally, the signs of that internal struggle had first become evident in an incident at Ipswich Town on August 31. When Ipswich equalised in the 78th minute a supporter banged his hand on the top of the Newcastle United dug-out in victory. It wasn't a premeditated attack but an almost involuntary reaction to scoring. That wasn't how Keegan saw it. Within the shelter the force of the blow caused one of the metal support struts inside to bang against his head. The outraged manager, rather theatrically holding his head, leapt out and confronted the supporter who had done it, grabbing him by the coat and pushing him around. The police were obliged to go in and calm the situation down. When he had recovered Keegan admitted, 'Maybe I was wrong to take things into my own hands. But it's not right that these things should happen.' Then he added, 'That was the best performance of our season.' The whole incident smacked of overreaction, but Keegan, perhaps embarrassed by the whole thing, attempted to turn it into a safety issue. 'Maybe the time has come to have a look at these dug-outs with plastic backs. It's something to be concerned about when you've got managers and players sitting in the dug-out with the crowd able to come in and punch through the top of it. I was leaning back with my head on the dug-out when Ipswich scored. The fan smashed his hand on it and I hit my head on the metal bar. Managers and coaches are vulnerable to this kind of action and it would be a good idea if there were more police around the dugouts. We've changed a lot of things like squad numbers and names on shirts but perhaps we need to go back and look at some basics like protecting the managers. I was just trying to do my job when some idiot came up and smashed me on the head through the box.' Presently Keegan called for the St James' Park dug-outs to be blacked out, saying, 'I don't see why people should be looking in.' The episode had the air of an extended tantrum and it is tempting to conclude that the real source of the anger lay in the words 'when Ipswich scored'.

Keegan's temper was to be tested again, and sooner than anyone could have imagined. Playing away at Southampton

Keegan, finding his side 1-0 down, decided to bring Lee Clark off. Clark, obviously upset at his manager's decision, let his petulance show and visibly complained as he came off the field, kicking out at the bench. Keegan's reaction was mesmerising, he leapt to his feet, grabbed Clark by the collar and shouted at him. It was as embarrassing as it was shocking.

There was to be more. Keegan had a particular theory of man management; he wanted his players to be well-rounded individuals who could represent the club well, men who were at ease with the media and who were happy to meet the public on behalf of the club. This he felt was a vital part of their development as players. 'I think it's important to explore every avenue. I always did as a player, I made records and people laughed, but it's a tremendous experience and I encourage the players to do different things apart from the normal charity stuff. We do encourage young players to go in pairs to presentations and stuff like that so they learn to meet people and learn to conduct themselves. We always send a senior player with them if we can and that way they learn the confidence and how they should dress and that sort of thing, and I think it's very important because there is more to life than football. You sometimes forget that when you are involved in it. But they have got to learn to be able to project themselves in all sorts of surroundings and all sorts of situations, and if they mature as a person they will probably become better footballers for it. They'll mature as footballers.'

It may have worked for Keegan, a punchy, white working-class lad from the north of England, but for others it was less easy and in particular Andy Cole was struggling to adapt to the requirements of life as a Newcastle player. The first signs of Andy Cole's problems emerged when the player disappeared before an away game in February at Wimbledon, spending time with his London friends.

Keegan was furious, although he claimed that there wasn't an argument. 'One of my objections was that his training wasn't good enough. But there was no row as such. If that was an argument then we have 20 of them every day of the week at this football club.' When Cole said he was homesick Keegan's response was, 'Then go home.' Yet although Keegan had a short temper he also had an understanding nature when it came to young players, and within two weeks he had softened. 'Because Andy Cole is such a complicated character we never really knew we had a problem until ten days ago. I'd been encouraging him to do interviews with various branches of the media to bring him out of his shell. But maybe it was wrong for him, for that I will take the blame. He's a smashing lad but we have got to accept that Newcastle, geographically, is a difficult move if you're not a Geordie. But to be fair, Robert Lee has shown it can be done and that it's possible to adjust. Andy is a single lad and this adds to the problem. He just needs to be left alone. Maybe we have got to look at what we do for players in terms of accommodation and that sort of thing when they move to the club. Maybe we have failed a little bit there. And maybe Andy can hide more in London. He doesn't feel he is in a goldfish bowl. We understand his problems and we will help to solve them.' Keegan's forgiveness might have reflected the fact that Newcastle had lost their previous three matches. 'I have no worries playing him tomorrow because the only problems he has caused on the field have been to defences.' So Cole was back in the side. The player restricted himself to saying, 'As far as I am concerned, the matter is over.'

And Keegan concluded, 'I'm paid to do a job here, not sit on the fence. I regret the incidents involving Andy Cole. The problems get bigger as the club gets bigger and we come under more public scrutiny. It hasn't been the best of weeks, though fighting relegation 18 months ago was worse. There's still a lot right with this club and at least we have been open and honest, and I don't think any young players will flaunt themselves at this club again.

'If nothing else all this will have taught Andy Cole one secret about football: if you have a problem never let it affect you on the pitch. I've been down the same road a million times so I know how he feels.'

October also saw Keegan further commit himself to Newcastle United, signing a new deal that was estimated to earn him £250,000 a year and seemingly put himself out of contention for the England manager's job. Keegan beamed, 'You'd need to be mental to want to walk away now. I'm staying until 1996 and I hope to be standing here in two or three years renewing my contract again. The speculation about England was flattering but it was fiction, not fact. It has not been a problem for me but it has affected people around me. Even the players have been affected by it.'

And, just in case Keegan was mental, Hall insisted, 'This gets rid of the uncertainty at Newcastle and puts Kevin among the best-paid managers in Britain. It is a straightforward contract with no escape.' But uncertainty would remain as the defining feature of Keegan's time at Newcastle whether Hall liked it or not.

With Cole resettled, he and Beardsley established a link that would, by the end of the season, be responsible for 65 goals in League and Cup competitions. Newcastle's football was increasingly characterised by its width, pace and excitement. All of which came to fruition on January 4 when Newcastle went to Norwich, another side noted for its desire to play good football rather than clogging its way to a success. Norwich went one goal up, but Newcastle responded with a brave display of passing and penetration that saw them win the game 1-2. Keegan was delighted by what he had witnessed: 'The best performance of my managerial career so far.'

February was to confront Keegan, once more, with the inability of all of his players to maintain his own high standards of commitment. After Newcastle lost a league match 4-2 at Wimbledon Keegan set the tone, 'If you can find a player that did himself justice then you are a better man than I am.' It was not then an occasion to be celebrated, which Keegan made explicitly clear to his players. Instead the squad were to go bowling with their manager. Understandably not everyone in the team regarded the prospect as a fun-filled one and that evening Barry Venison, Steve Howey and Alex Mathie went drinking in a wine bar.

When Keegan found out he reacted swiftly and decisively. Venison had his captaincy taken from him and given to Peter Beardsley, one of the bowlers, and all three players were fined by the club. Newcastle had lost in the league, been knocked out of the FA Cup by Luton Town and Keegan had had his authority publicly challenged again. Keegan responded by taking his family to Scotland for three days. The club was quick to deny that Keegan was suffering from the pressure of recent set-backs on the pitch. McDermott was left in charge and he explained, 'Kevin has been a little run-down. He wanted a break and he has gone to get out of the way. It has been arranged for some time. But he is in touch with the club every day to discuss things with me and in case anything develops on the transfer front.' Keegan was back for the Blackburn match on February 19. Newcastle lost.

February was not all gloom for Keegan as he spent a further £2.25 million of Hall's money on the Norwich player Ruel Fox, a winger who could play on either side of the pitch. Fox would provide another option for supplying the ball to Andy Cole, and Newcastle embarked upon a devastating return to form that saw them win ten matches, draw two and lose two in the last 14 Premiership matches of the season.

At the end of the season Newcastle finished third and qualified for Europe via the UEFA Cup. It was Keegan's great achievement; by adding Beardsley to Cole he had produced a team that was two places away from being the best in the land. The terror that they inspired was illustrated by the fact that Newcastle were awarded more penalties than any other Premiership side that season. Keegan looked forward to their run continuing. 'That was their first season together. I don't know whether Coley will score 40-odd goals again but he'll score plenty. Beardsley might get 40.'

But Newcastle had not won the Championship; Alex Ferguson's Manchester United had done that. Although honours were even over the season, it had been 1-1 in both Premiership encounters, Keegan and the rest of Newcastle knew it was the United on the other side of the north country that had to be beaten.

In May Keegan signed a new ten-year contract that seemed an irrefutable statement of his intent to stay with Newcastle. As he usually did on these occasions, he made a measured assessment of what Newcastle could go on to do. 'Newcastle United are going to be the biggest football club on the planet.' Keegan's title was changed to director of football and coaching, and he received a financial deal that would work out at £5 million over five years. Keegan was also rewarded with the arrival of his ex-manager at Newcastle, Arthur Cox. Keegan was famously weak as a tactical thinker, and having Cox alongside himself and McDermott would, as Keegan saw it, immensely strengthen Newcastle's bid to break Manchester United's dominance. It was obvious to followers of Keegan's career that he was putting in place his own version of the Liverpool bootroom, but more importantly Cox was a friend to Keegan and Keegan had talked warmly of him in the past.

'Arthur Cox was perhaps the main reason I decided to sign for them. Looking back now, there were, I suppose, two things which drew me to St James' Park, the size and stature of the club, and Arthur. In the end, most things in life do come down to people and the relationships you make and maintain. It is people you tie yourself to, not buildings or jobs. In footballing terms, Arthur and myself did not work together for all that long but they were valuable times for me and possibly for him as well. I learned a great deal from him and while we are totally different in many respects, we share a mutual respect for each other's abilities.'

With Cox by his side and the contract signed the country was obliged to accept that Keegan would never now become manager of England. Keegan had given up on the management job that ranks above all others.

'People who know me won't be surprised. They know if I have a chance of being successful I won't give it up. The England manager's job is never in my thoughts now. This is my England up here. You can't ask for any more commitment to Newcastle from myself, the directors and the players. This is a challenge. It's not something you can walk away from. Before this I had never signed a contract for more than three years. What's so exciting is that it's in our hands to take this club on a decade of real adventure...We have a structure to challenge Manchester United now. We can give them a run for their money.'

His remarks carried within them the seeds of his own downfall. Newcastle would challenge Manchester United, and fail. And Kevin Keegan would walk away from Newcastle United.

'Up pops the old devil'

Keegan must have started the 1994-95 season feeling that the Championship was his for the taking. 'Our aim is to win it, that's the next step. We had a good side last year. We will be very close to Manchester United, very close. We've know the capability of surprising other sides with the teams we put out. They know Cole and Beardsley are going to play but after that I've got so many permutations.' Those permutations were added to by the arrival of Philippe Albert and Marc Hottiger. Albert was a well-set defender, bought for £2.65 million from Belgian champions Anderlecht. A regular in the Belgian national squad, he was first noticed by Keegan during that summer's World Cup finals in the United States, as was Hottiger, Switzerland's right-back who came from FC Sion for £520,000. 'It would be a surprise if they didn't settle in this team easily, because we're as much a continental side as an English side.'

Keegan was able to temper his enthusiasm to a degree and he knew where Newcastle's weaknesses were. He always did, it was just that he was ill equipped to deal with them. 'I'm under no illusions. The next step, although a small one, is not going to be easy. We've made giant strides. We came up running from the First Division, then we looked very much at home in the Premiership. It has to be our aim to go two better than we did last season. A lot of hard work went into finishing third and I don't think the most ardent of fan of any other club would argue we weren't the third-best side. I think we were the country's most entertaining side. We'll continue to play that way but will try to add more steel and discipline needed to win the odd games when we don't hit our normal, flowing, one-touch football and when, say, Andy Cole and Peter Beardsley are not causing major problems for the defences. If we had a fault last season we didn't hang on and win games we should have won.'

That would always be Newcastle's weakness under Keegan, losing matches that they should have won, yet Keegan, rather than change tactics, would always look to buying better players as the solution to a problem that had more to with the system than the individuals. It was a response that left him open to allegations of buying his way to success, allegations he rejected. 'I don't think it's just a case of money when it comes to success now. It's a case of what clubs have, not what they can get. If you have quality you have to keep it. When you look in the market place you realise there's not much in the window. It's a great comfort that when players are available Newcastle can compete for them. Newcastle is now run as it should always have been. If we want something doing it's all in house to do it. Everyone is pulling the right way, everyone is ambitious. I'm very proud of what's been achieved and what's happening. Geordies come up and say, "Thanks, I can't believe what it's been like, the last year and a half." For years we'd been the whipping boys. Two years ago as we started my first full season, I said we wanted to do a Leeds, that is, not only win promotion but win the big title in our second Premiership season. That means this one. We could profit from Manchester United being in Europe. I know we're in the UEFA Cup, but for them there's the challenge of winning the European Cup so they can be compared with the great sides. The European Cup can be your biggest asset, but it can also nibble away at your squad, nibble way at the league. I'd say only five teams can win the Premiership title this time, the top three of last season, Arsenal and Leeds. It's not silly to put ourselves under pressure by going for the top. It's right for a club of our size, players and support.'

There was still only one team to beat. 'What Manchester United have on us is experience. They've won it before and all their players, apart from Steve Bruce, who probably should have been, are internationals. We're not at that stage yet but we're getting there. We're starting to get players in the England B squad and we've just bought two proven internationals. We came close to it last year and we've added some great players. Now we've got tremendous depth. Last year I felt Manchester United just had a better squad than us. As simple as that. They could withstand injuries. We were down to the boards at the end of the season.'

Once more Leicester City made an appearance in the Keegan story. They were Newcastle's first opponents of the season, and once more they were beaten, losing 3-1 to a Newcastle side that played with dazzling speed. Beardsley and Cole duly scored with

Robbie Elliot adding the third.

Newcastle were unstoppable – winning the opening six matches in a row whilst also finding time to announce their arrival in Europe with a joyous 5-0 defeat of Royal Antwerp in the UEFA Cup. A performance that approached the unbelievable in its audacity.

After the game Urbain Haessaert, the Antwerp coach, approached Keegan and said, 'Mr Keegan, I've never seen such quality football played at such a pace in all my life.' Keegan was taken aback. 'I was speechless, because that's what we work to do. It was the speed of our game that made them look what they weren't, pedestrian. I was just so wary of Europe, for some reason. People said I'd played there, but I wasn't going to Belgium to play. I kept hearing Europe was different. I read George Graham's article warning us not to be naive. I soaked it all up, thought it was all common sense, even considered using three centre-backs or a sweeper system, but decided we'd got where we are by playing a certain way. I always do in the end. It'll be the same at Arsenal.'

It was, as the next Saturday the best defence in the country found themselves broached by Newcastle's attack three times. Newcastle's own, less well-regarded defence let in two, but working on Keegan's theory of scoring more than you let in, it was all Newcastle needed. Whatever the match, Keegan wouldn't give up on his commitment to attacking football. 'We don't throw tactics out of the window, but at the end of the day I always come back to the same thing. I think, hold on, I didn't sign Peter Beardsley to tell him to track back. I didn't sign Ruel Fox to ask him to play any different from the way he did at Norwich. Or Robert Lee. I bought him because he's a talent. I'm not going to ask them to change. You go out and play and you take people on and you challenge them to play football and if you're better than them and you have a bit of luck, you get your reward.'

After the whistle blew on the 3-2 victory at Highbury Andy Cole stood in front of the travelling Newcastle supporters and kissed his shirt. Keegan was, along with the rest of the country, in awe of Cole's abilities. 'Andy took the Premiership by storm last season, breaking club records with 41 league and cup goals but he can improve on what he did. He's an exceptional talent playing with, in Peter, the perfect foil for him. They are as exciting a partnership as I've ever seen in this country. Andy set his standards in our last games in the First Division. He was bought while we were top, so the pressure was on him. But he showed his character. He really wants to play and he scores tremendous goals. Not long-range ones, but his are very varied. When a shot is parried or charged down who does the ball go to? Andy Cole.' But if Cole was the ideal striker, Beardsley was Keegan's epitome of the ideal player. 'Pedro' was his perfect professional, 'Enthusiasm is a word which comes to mind when I think of Peter. At 33 he remains youthful. We call him Peter Pan, and he'll be just as outstanding when the European Championships are here in 1996. He puts so much into training that if I didn't know him I'd be saying, "Save something for the game." He just goes out and enjoys it.'

Newcastle were a club transformed; they were top of the Premiership, dazzling Europe with their football and were, to use Sir John Hall's favourite word, 'magnificent'. And magnificent was the word for the new stadium which had risen up out of the old

Gallowgate. But the new stadium was not big enough to house all those on Tyneside who wanted to watch Newcastle play so even more fans were obliged to drive to Durham to see the team train. On one occasion 3,000 supporters turned up at Maiden Castle. When a couple of players tried to avoid the signing sessions, which could take up to half an hour, Keegan took them to task. The fans were the most important thing and this was all for them. 'A lot of clubs wouldn't do it. But I think in the north-east, and Newcastle in particular, when they can't get into matches, how else can they see their heroes? It's a pain in the backside some days, but the players have accepted it. If you're Andy Cole these are the people who buy your Reebok boots. And for the young lads coming in, it's become the norm. That's the way it is. I can do things here that other clubs might think are crazy.'

If Keegan was happy to expose himself and the team, he proved to be less open with the press. Angered by a report in Newcastle's morning newspaper, the *Journal*, that the club had been less than honest about the fitness of the players, he promptly got the club to stop all communications with the paper. It was the season's first loss of temper. The second came within days. Keegan, newly appointed as the manager of England's U-21 side, got so annoyed with the referee when Robbie Fowler was sent off in a 3-1 defeat of Austria that officials were forced to order him to sit down.

Newcastle's dream start came to an end on October 29 and the bogey-man who woke them up was Alex Ferguson. Newcastle entered Old Trafford unbeaten in the Premiership, they left 2-0 losers. On top of that illustration of Ferguson's ability to deflate Keegan's ambitions, Newcastle's manager had also to cope with more problems with Andy Cole. This time they were physical. Cole developed shin splints and was out for five weeks. If Keegan had complained of his player's commitment in the past, he now praised. 'We have abused him. I'm not going to do that any further. He wants to play, he's never stopped trying, but you can see how much it's hurting. He is struggling to do the basic things which are natural to a player of his ability. It's up to me to tell him to stop.'

For most of November and December Newcastle were third in the Premiership, but they had stopped winning, only beating QPR and Leicester in the whole two months, and they were also knocked out of the Coca-Cola Cup by Manchester City. This loss of form coupled with their European defeat by Bilbao caused unease at the club, and the press, so recently championing Newcastle's open football, turned on Keegan. Was he good enough after all? Keegan chose to meet the criticism head on.

'People have the right to kick us where it hurts. If I was outside the club I would probably be saying the same thing, that the bubble at Newcastle has burst. But I want my players to react to the criticism and I want it to hurt them. I want them to react positively to criticism. It's easy to react to the plaudits, "You're a great player, it's great you are in the England squad." That's the easy bit. I'm looking to see what my players do when people start to leave Newcastle out of any talk of the Premiership title race. If, as an outsider, I had seen us playing over the last month, I would leave us out as well. When you look at the predictions for the honours next May the only mention we get are "not good enough" or "dropping away". Maybe that will prove to be a good thing. I thrive on pressure but there is no reason to believe that every player at your club thrives on it. Maybe it has been getting to some of the players. Let's not forget that the last 12 months have been a real adventure. In a way we are still the new kids on the block. The last month, in which we have struggled, has hurt me. But I'm realistic enough to know we have travelled a long journey in a short time. I accept that people are entitled to ask questions of us. We have had a bad spell, yet we are still in striking distance of the leaders. We have talked and analyzed things a lot. But the only chance of us winning anything is through the same players who have got us up here, the same players who have had a dodgy month. We have to get back to doing what we are good at. We are a passing team. We will never be long-ball merchants or scrappers. We haven't assembled that type of player here. If our football isn't flowing, we are in trouble. We're not able to grind out results. If it goes for us we are the best team in the country. The minute it stops, and when we have to get a result by scrambling a goal, we struggle.'

Talk now began about Keegan's ability to handle the pressure of the job. His hair was now plainly greyer than it had been, his demeanour often hunched and unhappy, but Keegan claimed to be well. 'I still enjoy this job. In fact it makes your job a bit more interesting when you have injuries and when things aren't quite as good. When you think that everything in the garden is rosy, up pops the old devil. I get frustrated, but I am not someone who throws cups about. I am more of a manager who will pull players aside for a quiet word and tell them they have more to offer. Is there a problem? Is their family OK? I take a close look at the individual's training. But honestly I blame myself for what has happened recently. I pick the team. I have chosen to change it at odd times. Sometimes it has been forced on me, but occasionally it was changed purely by me. Now I must get us out of this pickle.'

On January 10 an astonished Tyneside found out just how Keegan intended to get out of the pickle – he sold Andy Cole. There was a sense of disbelief in the city, he may not have scored for nine matches and he may have been plagued by shin splints but how on earth could Keegan have sold one of his best players, and to, of all places, Manchester United? Conceivably the only thing that could have been worse would have been Keegan selling Cole to local rivals Sunderland. For the first time Keegan's judgement was openly doubted by many of the Toon Army, there was talk of betrayal, the old fear that Newcastle were a selling team still lurked in the heart of every Newcastle supporter; the sale of Cole seemed to be awful proof that it was true.

It was in this atmosphere that Keegan showed just how strong his character was and also that his commitment to Newcastle's supporters wasn't lip-service but a deeply held belief. Or conversely he reacted as he always did when he thought his integrity was being challenged – he went on the attack.

It was a scene that couldn't be imagined at any other football club or with any other football manager. Keegan came out on to the steps at the back of the Milburn stand and, obviously agitated, he addressed the fans, 'I know how much Andy Cole means to you, but my job is to make decisions for this club. This is a once in a lifetime offer which I don't think would come at any other time from any other club...you've got to let me do that.

If it doesn't work I know what the implications are, I know what the bottom line is.'

Twenty-four hours later Hall spoke, 'None of you have any reason to doubt Kevin Keegan or me. We've taken the club from nothingness, we're on course to becoming the one of the top three in the UK, the top ten in Europe. Life's all about decisions and you shouldn't need me to tell you Kevin's ability in the market and motivation of players is second to none. We are backing him because he knows what he is doing.'

Keegan insisted that the decision had been a footballing one and not financially motivated. His logic was simple: a Newcastle attack based on Andy Cole had been found out and that was why they had stopped winning. Most Premiership clubs had worked out how to shackle Newcastle's style and unless it was changed then Newcastle would not win the Premiership. The deal also involved Newcastle getting Manchester United's exciting young winger Keith Gillespie, a player who would be well suited to the pace and verve of Newcastle's game, if of course, Newcastle could rediscover it. However, the team only won seven of their remaining Premiership fixtures, and finished sixth at the end of the season that Keegan and Hall had marked down as a championship-winning one.

As if that wasn't bad enough, the player Newcastle had earmarked to take over from Andy Cole, Paul Kitson, scored only four more goals. Keegan had not emulated Howard Wilkinson's achievement at Leeds United, he had not even qualified for Europe.

'It really has got to me'

In the summer of 1995 Kevin Keegan put his hand in Sir John Hall's pocket and, in the words of Viv Nicholson, began to 'Spend, spend, spend'. On June 3 defender Warren Barton was bought for £4 million from Wimbledon, four days later Keegan paid Queens Park Rangers £6 million for their centre forward Les Ferdinand, and on July 6 Keegan acquired the man who would be both one of his most exasperating and rewarding players, when he paid Paris Saint Germain £2.5 million for the beautiful but flawed talents of the left-winger David Ginola.

Kevin Keegan may well look back on August 1995 as one of the best months of his life; it was certainly the month in which all he hoped for, all that he had believed was possible for Newcastle United, looked to be happening. Newcastle went through the month winning all four of their Premiership games. By the time goalkeeper Shaka Hislop arrived in August Keegan had spent £40 million on building a side. When the first game of the season kicked-off all four of his new players were in the starting line-up and the supporters were desperate to see what they would bring to the team. Appropriately the game was at home, and the first league game inside Hall's pleasure dome brought Coventry as visitors on a day of sunshine and, for Newcastle, success. But it was Newcastle's more established talents that won the game for Keegan. Gillespie was on devastating form and he completed a sprint down the wing with the perfect cross for Robert Lee to head in. The second goal came from a typically audacious run in the box by Peter Beardsley who, after he was clipped as he entered the six-yard box, stood up and scored the penalty. And things were rounded-off in style when Les Ferdinand scored a third.

St James' Park was frighteningly triumphant, the flashes of white on the thousands of replica shirts reflecting the bright sunlight made the eyes blink. Keegan and McDermott in matching white tops and black tracksuit bottoms which made them look like they had been dressed by their mothers, gambolled and jumped along the sidelines each time Newcastle scored. Caught in the sun, they were two-tone flashes of joy against a St James' Park pitch that had never looked greener. For a moment the management team stopped being the management team and became themselves supporters.

It was Newcastle's second game, a trip to Bolton Wanderers, that showed the accuracy of Keegan's vision in buying Ginola. Completely at ease with Newcastle's swift attacking, Ginola ran his line and baffled any Bolton player who came near him, rendering them lumpen by his presence. Suddenly the logic in Keegan's purchases made clear and irrefutable sense. Ginola beat his marker and crossed directly to Ferdinand in the Bolton penalty area who, making himself taller than he had the right to be, met the ball clean and hard with his head. But just in the moment when Newcastle seemed to be in the ascendancy they were brought back to earth and exposed as a team who still possessed an inherent flaw. A Bolton corner left the entire Newcastle defence in a quandary of their own making; as Gudni Bergsson leapt and sent a header toward goal, Barton remained still. Confused and grounded, he watched the ball travel into the Newcastle net, having as little effect on its delivery or progress as any of the watching crowd.

Keegan slumped but this was to be one of those occasions when the sheer force of Newcastle's attacking football would make up for the inadequacy, or plain incompetence, in defence. Newcastle merely pressed even harder, and before the match was over Les Ferdinand scored again and Robert Lee added a third. Ferdinand's goal was so supremely good, such a one-man triumph over what appeared to be the entire Bolton defence that worries about Newcastle's own weak defence were temporarily forgotten, although they would be back.

The following match at Sheffield Wednesday was remarkable. Not only did it provide the third win in a row for Newcastle but it also revealed David Ginola to be in possession of a devastating ability to cut in from the wing and, instead of crossing to Les Ferdinand, shoot into the right-hand corner of the goal, giving the keeper the opportunity to do nothing more than flap at the ball comically as it passed him by. Ginola, hand still swathed in white bandage from an earlier injury, became in that instant the most glamorous player in the country. Keegan's pleasure was compounded by Beardsley scoring and the prospect of beating Middlesbrough when they came to St James' Park, which Newcastle duly did. This time when Ginola worked his way in from the right, although work is the wrong verb for a task he appeared to accomplish effortlessly, he again found Ferdinand who once scored with his head.

At the end of August Newcastle were at the top of the Premiership and unbeaten. They were still at the top of the Premiership at the end of the year with only three teams having managed to beat them in the league. Newcastle had established themselves with a lead that seemed unassailable.

But it was to be two cup encounters that signalled the demise of Newcastle's season. A two-match encounter with Chelsea in the FA Cup ended at St James' Park when the London side won on penalties. Newcastle were then knocked out of the Coca-Cola Cup by Arsenal on January 10 at Highbury, and Keegan's hot temperament came to a boil in a touchline row with Arsenal's manager Bruce Rioch. David Ginola was sent off and, to the surprise of onlookers, things got so involved between Keegan and Rioch, with McDermott joining the fray as well, that the police had to get involved to break the situation up.

Although Manchester United were getting on with the job of winning matches, the attention stayed firmly fixed on Keegan, and his latest addition to the Newcastle squad, Faustino Asprilla. Keegan had been chasing the Columbian international and Parma player for some time, and he arrived at St James' Park to be met by a flurry of snow and a storm of media interest. Keegan said, 'We were determined to get him,' and Hall added, with only the slightest hint of exasperation in his voice, 'Kevin's rated him highly for a long time and Kevin's got his man. As I've said many times, he's good for Newcastle and he's very good for the Premier League.' In his first game Asprilla made a goal, a particularly sweet one for Newcastle, as not only did it result from a dribble on the wing that left the defence scratching their heads but importantly for the fans, it was against Middlesbrough.

Yet some could not understand Keegan's decision to alter a squad that seemed almost certain to win the Premiership, and of all the players to get, Asprilla was the most disturbing imaginable. Although he regularly baffled the opposition, he had a similar effect on his own side at times. Asprilla's second match for Newcastle, away at West Ham, was the moment when the side's league form faltered. They lost 2-0 and although they would win again, Newcastle never looked as confident. At Upton Park they began to worry the Championship away.

The last agonizing weeks of Keegan's 1996 Premiership campaign eked away at his physical and psychological strength. If there was one point where the country and Keegan realised that they wouldn't catch Manchester United it was when Stan Collymore scored Liverpool's injury-time winner in the 4-3 defeat at Anfield on April 3.

Keegan was caught for ever in the nation's imagination, hand on his head, eyes closed, dropping in despair behind the advertising hording, down and out.

The match earned the dubious title Match of the Decade before the evening's coverage on Sky TV had even finished.

Cataclysmically and almost inevitably, Newcastle had capitulated. They had visibly come down a gear since equalising and towards the end of the match looked as though they had decided that enough honour had been earned by both sides just for participating in such an exciting and extended encounter, that a draw was the only fair way to settle it. Stan Collymore wasn't thinking like that.

Keegan, as ever, sought solace in the fact that his side, and he, had done the right thing. They had gone to Anfield and played open expansive football that had dazzled the world for an hour and a half. The next day Keegan received a personal telegram from the chairman of UEFA congratulating him on the way Newcastle had played. Suddenly the whole purpose of football had been forgotten, it was no longer to win but to entertain. If Keegan couldn't win on the pitch with the style of football Newcastle were playing then he would win off it. Denied victory by the calm thinking of Stan Collymore, Keegan went looking for a moral victory on the nation's air waves and the back pages of the press. Liverpool manager Roy Evans knew it was all illusory; he was the only man to leave the ground who wasn't gasping with pleasure, for unlike Keegan, he knew there had been only one winner that night, Alex Ferguson, the brooding presence 30 miles up the East Lancs Road. Roy Evans came out after the match and said, 'We can't play like that, it was suicidal. That isn't what football is about.'

But it was the only way Keegan knew how to play, it was either that or he went. Any good fortune Newcastle could have expected went to everyone but them. As if the events at Anfield hadn't been enough, Newcastle fans had to endure another cruel blow at Blackburn. Newcastle, ahead by a goal, looked on for a win until Rovers' Geordie, Graham Fenton, scored twice, and in doing so virtually ensured the championship went to Old Trafford.

As Ferguson tightened his grip on the Premiership he indulged in an increasingly offensive trickle of personal and general swipes which seemed aimed at unsettling Keegan. As the Newcastle manager chose to ignore Ferguson's comments, most of the football world didn't suspect that they were having an effect on Keegan. Then one night everybody found what up until then only those who were closest to him must have known: Ferguson's comments had angered him.

The Manchester United manager had intimated that Leeds and Nottingham Forest would not try to beat Newcastle as hard as they would try to overcome Manchester United. After going to Elland Road and defeating Leeds Keegan finally cracked, and when he did the contents of his troubled psyche spilled out into the nation's pubs and front rooms via the startled and half-comprehending questioning of Sky Television's Andy Gray and Richard Keys.

Keegan: 'I think you've got to send Alec Ferguson a tape of this game, haven't you? Isn't that what he asked for?'

Gray: 'Well I'm sure if he was watching it tonight, Kevin, he could have no arguments about the way Leeds went about their job and really tested your team.'

Keegan: 'And...and we...we're playing Notts Forest on Thursday and...he objected to that! Now that was fixed up four months ago. We f...supposed to play Notts Forest. I mean, that sort of stuff, we...is...it's been...we're bet...We're bigger than that.'

Richard Keys: 'But that's part and parcel of the psychology of the game, Kevin, isn't it?'

Gray: 'No, I don't think so.'

Keegan: 'No! When you do that, with footballers, like he said about Leeds. And when you do things like that about a man like Stuart Pearce...I...I've kept really quiet but I'll tell ya something, he went down in my estimation when he said that. We have not resorted to that. But I'll tell ya you can tell him now if you're watching this. We're still fighting for this title and he's got to go to Middlesbrough and get something and...and...I'll tell ya honestly I will love it if we beat them...Love it!'

Keys: 'Well, quite plainly the message is, it's a long way from over and you're in there still scrapping and battling and you'll take any of these just as long as you continue to get the results?'

Keegan, [paying no attention to Keys at all]: 'I...I think football in this country is so honest and so...Honestly, when you look sometimes abroad, you've got your doubts. But it really has got to me and I...I...I've voiced it live, not in front of the press or anywhere, I'm not even going to the press conference. But the battle's still on and Man United have not won this yet!'

It wasn't so much an outburst as a haemorrhage. The non-partisan wheeled backwards from the TV, what on earth was Keegan doing? Pundits solemnly announced that his marbles had rolled away for ever, but in the north-east the reaction was far different. The Scots have always been the enemy just over the way, and Ferguson by his unfortunately sour-faced demeanour, his perceived lack of goodwill and his inability, or unwillingness to take fair criticism or offer justified praise to other sides, was hated on Tyneside. The fans were outraged by Ferguson, that their manager was as well was natural to them and it further confirmed that he was one of them. At times in the interview Keegan could hardly get his words out he was so cross. Cheating was the one allegation that Keegan was unable to hear without losing his temper. And as Keegan saw it, Ferguson was suggesting that he was cheating.

Drawing away at Nottingham Forest in effect ended Newcastle's realistic chances of winning the Premiership. The last day of the season presented Keegan with an almost impossible task: it wasn't just that his side had to beat Tottenham Hotspur at St James', they were also dependent on Middlesbrough beating Manchester United at the Riverside Stadium. United didn't seem to be playing a team that was willing to give its all. Against a Middlesbrough side managed by ex-Manchester United captain Brian Robson and with fans whose only comfort after a disappointing season was to see Newcastle fail, anything but victory was never likely. In Newcastle itself hope lived eternal, and even if every soul in the city knew that the Championship would inexorably go to Manchester that day, they suspended any belief in the likelihood of failure and instead opted for having a fiesta in their city. The media poured into Tyneside, every pub seemed to have its own TV crew. The streets were lost in a throb of black and white, the Three Bulls Pub on Percy Street around the corner from the ground was draped completely in a giant banner. Everywhere good humour abounded. By the time of the kick off an atmosphere more suited to winning a championship than losing it had taken over St James' Park. The atmosphere was rendered all the stranger by the knowledge that events would be decided 40 miles away at the Riverside Stadium.

Keegan addressed the task ahead in the match programme, 'We can win the title if we beat Tottenham this afternoon, but only if Manchester United also lose at Middlesbrough. That's the disappointment, that we're not in control of our own destiny. As ever, we will set about our task in a positive manner. You can ponder as long as you like on what might have been at Forest on Thursday – you can say you had some bad luck or that you didn't get the rub of the green – but the record books will show that the result was 1-1 and that it left us two points adrift of Manchester United with one game to play. It was major disappointment – there's no disguising that – but it's over. Our destiny won't be decided by Ian Woan's equaliser at Forest, or by any other single incident in one game. The season lasts 38 matches and the team that finishes top will finish there strictly on merit. I've always believed that and I've seen nothing this season to persuade me to change my mind. Everybody connected with this club – every fan and every neutral up and down the country – will have their own interpretation as to why one club won or lost it. My own feelings are that I'll be desperately disappointed if we're runners-up, because I believed from day one that we could be champions. We can still be, but if it's Manchester United I'll be the first to send their players a telegram of congratulations. They're the only team to have beaten us at St James' Park and, of course, they also beat us at Old Trafford. Our players have given us their best shot and if, in the final analysis, it's not been quite good enough then you have to pay tribute to the team that has been better. I said when I came here just over four years ago that I would try to give Newcastle United a team as good as their fans and I do think we are very close to that now. Your support has been fantastic and we – players and staff – are very grateful for it. The travelling fans are often different people from the St James' Park season ticket holders – often those who never see us play here because they can't get in. We have been lifted and inspired by our fabulous home support. We need one more inspired performance this afternoon. It could, after all, make us champions.'

It didn't. All Newcastle could ask of themselves was that they beat Tottenham Hotspur. But that task was to prove to be beyond them.

It was over. Newcastle had lost a 12-point lead, not only had they succumbed to what was ultimately the better side, but Keegan had himself lost out in one of the most intense psychological conflicts British football had seen since Alex Ferguson's previous prolonged battle with Kenny Dalglish. It is noteworthy that Keegan only mentioned sending a telegram of congratulations to the Manchester United players.

Keegan knew he had failed personally so he was all the more moved then when the Gallowgate crowd demanded his presence on the pitch. The chant of 'Keegan, Keegan' resounded again around the stadium just as it had in the pre-John-Hall St James' Park in 1982. The team ran a full circuit of the pitch, saluting each corner of the crowd, Keegan walked more slowly, contemplatively. By his side, as ever, walked Terry McDermott, the man who would do anything for his master. Keegan looked up to the bellowing crowd and surely the oft-repeated cliché about Newcastle fans came to him again, 'Imagine what they would be like if they won something'. The moment seemed too intense for Keegan, he didn't cry openly but his eyes were full. Perhaps it was then that he decided to go, the burden of being worshipped, of constantly being forgiven and allowed another crack at it but never quiet getting there had become an inescapable circle for him; perhaps in that moment Kevin Keegan knew he would never give the supporters what they deserved and that there wasn't enough of himself left to give as compensation any more.

As Keegan left the pitch, Newcastle's particularly annoying public announcer urged us all to come back next season. Few realised it would be Keegan's last, most gruelling encounter with the championship. With hindsight when he failed to overcome Tottenham Hotspur that day it would have been a more fitting time to go, but like natural full backs, Keegan couldn't recognise a natural full stop. His boss as ever had his mind on greater projects.

For Sir John Hall nothing could get in the way of what he had planned for Newcastle United. Even before the match, he was putting a millennial spin on Newcastle's likely failure to win the Championship. 'For me, today is a celebration, whatever the result, whatever our immediate destiny. A celebration of a terrific season, of football played in the most thrilling and exciting way, and in the right spirit. As we move towards the millennium let's be the team, and the club, that dominates the millennium!'

As Keegan walked around St James' Park in a state of existential nausea, Sir John was thinking big again. 'This is just the beginning. The best is yet to come. Newcastle United are well and truly on the soccer map and I am supremely confident that we will go on to become a dominant force in both British and European football. We are back in Europe next season, and what a joy that is to contemplate. As I look ahead I see such an exciting future. This club can be the biggest and best in the United Kingdom. It's our mission statement to become just that.' Hall cannot speak or write without sounding like he is issuing a share prospectus, and in this case that was exactly what he was doing. Hall knew the club had to go public so he had their failure to win anything neatly hidden behind what they would win. But promises mean even less in football than they do in business. Newcastle had failed and that could not be allowed to continue.

Hall added a coda that hinted as much, 'We've always known that the psychological barrier we had to break was to win something. And we also knew, from the time we entered the Premier League, that it was just a matter of time before we put some silverware on our table. As I say, we came a long way together in the last four years. The changes – on and off the pitch – have been dramatic. But I assure you that the plans for the next four or five years are even more dramatic.'

For Hall it was no longer unthinkable that Keegan should go; they may have come a long way together in the last four years, but it didn't mean that they had to stay together.

'Tinkering with a tremendous armoury'

Summers inevitably end brightly in football, the few months before England is enveloped in winter is a time when the previous year's failures are put in a new perspective. What two months before had been dashed hope becomes instead a platform for building on, failure is reassessed as coming close, and the year ahead becomes the fabled 'this time'. Keegan had ended the season padding around a St James' Park that was once more saluting the second-best; moved though he was, at the time he had let his impatience show through, 'I am fed up of going around the ground without a trophy and getting a fantastic ovation.'

Summer is also, of course, a time for strengthening a side, for considering the squad, perhaps adding to it and for letting weaker players go. However, in Keegan's case it was not always the weaker players that went. He had been forgiven on Tyneside for the sale of Andy Cole to Manchester United; Cole's initial failure to find any form at Old Trafford had lent the appearance of an astute move to the deal that had brought Newcastle £6 million and the winger Keith Gillespie. But any supporter who knew what Keegan was considering that summer would have been hard put to forgive the manager. Keegan was flirting with the idea of selling David Ginola.

Ginola, mercurial and untamed, had always chaffed under the rule of a man who was a bigger personality than any of his star players. He had seen the Championship and a chance of a European Champions League place lost, a particularly hard blow for a player desperate to impress since the battle at Highbury. So dispirited and personally affronted had he been at Dixon's and the referee's treatment of his brilliance that day that for the rest of the season he seemed to be resentfully holding back on it, deciding that it was too precious to be spoiled by the hurly burly of English football.

It is a mark of Ginola's game that he plays when he wants to. While he was never going to be happy to run back and defend he can at times be inspirational, cutting through the wing before turning in to shoot in the top right-hand corner of the net or set up another player; at others he can be almost unbearably annoying, running himself into trouble when all he need do is release the ball to a teammate. Ultimately he is a luxury rather than a necessity.

For Keegan no player was sacred and when Bobby Robson's Barcelona asked about the Frenchman, he listened. That Ginola stayed in the end was a mere matter of money, Ginola was 29 and, as Robson put it, 'Newcastle wanted too much money for him at his age.' Robson was not willing to spend the asking price, but the message had been made clear, anyone would go if Newcastle were so inclined. When the rumour of a Barcelona offer for Ginola became public knowledge Keegan was quick to refer to history in his explanation of events. Knowing the paranoid mentality that lurked in every Newcastle fan who had seen Waddle, Gascoigne and Beardsley sold and themselves sold down the river, he declared publicly, 'We knew of Barcelona's interest, but I maintain there is no way they are bigger than us. We will play in the same European cup competition this season and we have the same spending power. They wanted David when we bought him. We beat them then and we will do so again. There was a time when that would not have happened to a Newcastle player, a time when clubs like Barcelona could dictate to us. But we are no longer a selling club. There is more chance of us taking one of Barcelona's players than them getting one of ours.'

If Barcelona had come away from their failed bid for Ginola feeling that Newcastle were penny pinching then the next few weeks were to show them, and the entire football world, as the summer before had, that when they wanted Newcastle could be as spendthrift as a drunk lottery winner in Debenhams. When Newcastle United left for a pre-season tour of the Far East Keegan pulled out of the trip at the last minute. He had business to do.

When Keegan did arrive in Bangkok he made the business public. 'My hope is, and it will never be easy as there'll be problems along the way, my hope is to try and keep everybody happy, try and keep the squad together and obviously try and get the mentality of the payers a little more like the Europeans, of the

Italian style where you have big squads, AC Milan is a very good example. International players accept the fact that they're not being dropped but being they're being rested.'

Why should Newcastle players need consoling about losing their places before the season had even begun? The answer was arriving in the Far East as well. Surrounded by blue-shirted security police the most famous footballer in England emerged from the throng as a Newcastle United player. Keegan had signed Alan Shearer from Blackburn Rovers.

Earlier that summer, Euro '96 had come to grief for England as a matter of course with the inevitable failure to beat Germany, but the journey to the semi-final defeat at Wembley had seen Shearer find his national goal-scoring form again. Keegan had been interested in Alan Shearer before, but then who hadn't? Shearer had converted goal scoring from an art into an occupation; he did it by dint of determination, demonstrating an almost disdainful ability to get goals. Some of them were tap-ins and others were driven from outside the area, but, crucially, when he was amidst the opposition defence it did not occur to him that he would not score, consequently he often appeared to produce a goal from a situation where scoring seemed simply not an available option.

Since Kenny Dalglish had relinquished the manager's job at Blackburn and the side had slumped after winning the Premiership in 1995 it was obvious to most that Shearer would not be staying in that part of Lancashire for long. Although there had been interest in Italy the obvious place for Shearer to move to was on the same side of the Pennines, but Shearer had turned down

Manchester United before and to Geordie delight he did it again.

Few footballers are sentimentalists. They have very little time to make as much money as possible and they can't afford to let feelings for their home town get in the way of achieving the best deal possible. That's why Newcastle had waved goodbye to Beardsley and Gascoigne in the past. The club had seldom put its money where its mouth was. Yet in choosing his home town Newcastle, Shearer was turning his back on a definite European Champions League campaign with Manchester United.

It was said that Jack Walker would not let Shearer go to Manchester United; if he had done so his own supporters, grateful though they were for the Walker's steel money that had turned them into the big club that by rights they shouldn't have been, would have turned their fury on him. There was only one club who were well placed to benefit from Walker being shackled by inter-Lancastrian communal hatred.

Once more the outside of St James' Park became a place of public adulation, wearing the black and white striped shirt the fans had hardly dared dream that they would see him in, Shearer smiled his slightly gormless smile at the throng and waved awkwardly. And once more Newcastle made the national news, only this time it wasn't the usual bleak vista of thousands of disappointed Geordies holding their heads but thousands of them celebrating. Alan Shearer may have been happy to go back to the city he hadn't lived in for almost 11 years but it could be argued that at £15 million he probably would have been happy to play for anyone.

Football often claims to be dealing in the momentous and

this was perhaps an occasion when the claim was a justifiable one. The press conference reflected the size of the news, taking place on the St James' Park pitch facing the Milburn Stand. Sir John Hall could hardly contain himself, and before Shearer was introduced he delivered yet another version of his now-familiar line, 'This great club...a great day...the development of this club...the last four years.' After that litany of what were in effect excuses for not yet winning the Championship, Hall used the opportunity to plug the new stadium he was desperate for and the 'Soccer Academy' that would ensure that the Alan Shearers of the future were not lost to minnows like Southampton. Throughout Hall's spiel Keegan sat quietly, a smile played on his lips but he appeared fatigued rather than smug. Almost as an afterthought Hall mentioned his manager, noting that the success, such as it was, had been 'built under Kevin'.

Keegan would get his chance to talk, but first he stood and applauded with the assembled press and Newcastle Brewery employees who were jammed into a section of the Milburn Stand as Shearer came up on to the podium.

There was by now a standard script to be used on these occasions, and Shearer stuck to it. Hall's Geordie nation must be saluted, the money, the dealing, the contracts, the persuaders could all be hidden behind that. The real stuff of business in Keegan and Hall's world was always obscured by the hyperbole of their overblown folklore. Shearer, a man supposedly as slow to talk as he was quick to score, played his part well. 'Nothing should surprise me with the fans of Newcastle, but the reception that has been given to me certainly has done, and if any club or supporters deserve success then it's this club and hopefully I'll help with the rest of the players to try and bring that to them.'

In the press there was much talk of whether the sheer size of the figure involved would have any effect on the player's personality, it was in answering this point that Shearer's played his master stroke: 'It won't change me. After all I'm only a sheet-metal worker's son from Newcastle.' Dripping with irony it might have been, but the perfect press quote it certainly was. Hall was positively beaming. Now Keegan took his turn. The fans' ancient grudges were addressed first: 'We've sold 'em off time and time again up here. We've built stands with the money people have saved, and we've tried to buy other players to replace them quickly. That's gone at this club now. He's come here because he knows he had a great chance of winning something. Even with the great players we've got, this guy is going to improve them.' Even in that moment there was an uneasy sense that Keegan had brought Newcastle the one player they wanted more than any other, but had himself been divorced, or at least partially separated from the club.

Shearer's first goal for Newcastle duly came a few days later in a friendly at Lincoln City. It was only a penalty but no one takes penalties as well as Alan Shearer. Hall, Keegan and Newcastle needed the goal machine to start paying his dividend from the very beginning, so up stepped Shearer to shoot past the hapless lower-division keeper and the tills opened wide.

Newcastle's next match took them to Anderlecht. As a taster of the forthcoming UEFA Cup campaign it was more than encouraging for Keegan that his team won 2-1. Ginola scored and Shearer had a goal disallowed, but the game posed selection problems with the form of Faustino Asprilla, who showed what he could do when he wanted, scoring Newcastle's second goal and playing with a style that openly cocked a snoop at Keegan's talk of AC Milan and big squads.

The jubilation amongst the supporters and directors of the club at Shearer's capture wasn't a luxury Keegan allowed himself to hang on to. Apart from his personal demons he was well aware, if no one else was, that the moody figure of Alex Ferguson was about to loom into view. The 1996 Charity Shield caught the attention of the public more than any since 1974, when again it had been Keegan who had a personal showdown. On that occasion it was due to his scuffle with Billy Bremner but this time there was a bigger fight on the bill – a return to cudgels with Ferguson. Mindful of the fact that Newcastle's relationship with Manchester United was turning into a fierce battle, Keegan attempted to calm the atmosphere before the game, telling the press, 'It has been a long wait but on Saturday we get our chance to settle a few scores. Not physically, not brutally, not by kicking lumps out of people. But if we can beat Manchester United in the Charity Shield at Wembley it will be the massive kick-start our season needs.' There was to be no massive kick-start.

The Charity Shield was a match between the peoples' champions and the actual champions. A contest between Manchester United's hard-nosed and cynical appreciation of what needed to be done and the almost witless dash that characterised so much of Newcastle's play. On the day Newcastle didn't even manage the dash. Les Ferdinand had put aside his personal pride and consented to Shearer being given the totemic Newcastle number 9 shirt. And, as Shearer stepped on to the Wembley pitch in the number that had been stencilled on the backs of Jackie Milburn and Hughie Gallacher, the Geordies allowed themselves to believe that this was to be the moment of revenge against the great enemy. Instead they were obliged to witness a headless performance by Newcastle and four goals by Manchester United. Once more the Newcastle defence betrayed any progress the attack could make against a Manchester United side who were playing with all the effectiveness and arrogance that marks the club apart from the rest of England.

Apart from a Les Ferdinand shot towards the end of the first half, Newcastle spent the first 45 minutes gazing on as Manchester used space Newcastle hadn't even thought to fill. Keegan's half-time talk was enough to force Newcastle into coming forward in the second half and for a while they looked as if they might prevent the inevitable.

The much vaunted Shearer première was disastrous; quiet and seemingly out of sorts, at no point did he look likely to make a difference. On the one occasion Les Ferdinand was in a position to head down a ball to Shearer for what would have been a relatively easy chance, Ferdinand appeared to either deliberately ignore or, worse still, not see Shearer. The whole affair was humiliating, especially when Beckham lobbed Pavel Srincek. Once again the supporters were confronted with the fact that believing was not enough. Keegan had also been confronted by the fact but he has the ability to be almost jaunty in defeat and it was a re-animated manager who detailed what had gone wrong that afternoon. 'We were abysmal, dreadful. There looked to be a massive gulf between the sides today. I just hope the gulf is not as big as it looked. You could say anything critical about my team today and I would have to agree. We could not pass the ball, our work rate did not match theirs. Faustino Asprilla came on and did more in five minutes than most of the others did in 90. The only consolation for me is that we can't be that bad again. Alan Shearer will get better, and so will his partnership with Les Ferdinand.' It was ironic that the player that Keegan had insisted on buying and the player credited with losing Newcastle the Championship should be the only one, in Keegan's opinion, to come out of the Charity Shield with any credit. The other even more expensive signing, Shearer, was let off reasonably lightly after an afternoon in which he did not contrive to shoot at the goal directly until injury time.

'Strikers need service and nobody gives better service than Keith Gillespie, and I started with him on the bench. I put the team out, I was wrong. The lads on the bench will be thinking that they can get into the team now, instead of the players on the field making sure that the shirts are their own. People who say we bottled it last season will be saying we have bottled it again. I know there is plenty of work to be done.'

Musing that at least they 'couldn't get any worse' is hardly the ideal state of mind with which to embark upon a fresh challenge for the Championship, but the coming season could well be harder for all the expectation that was being loaded on to it, and if any good came out of the Charity Shield fiasco it was that Newcastle's potential was put into perspective. Not everyone knew just how hard it was going to be. Keegan, sucked dry of his enthusiasm and carrying the doubt ever since the last day of the previous season that it was worthwhile carrying on with Newcastle, was obliged to find some way of pulling these disparate disappointments into a psychologically coherent approach to the coming battle. If the defence was at sixes and sevens, then so was Keegan's mind.

The first Premiership game of the season, at Everton, illustrated just how difficult things were going to be. Everton are one of the Premiership's least attractive and least deserving sides, yet they contrived to beat what, theoretically, was a much more talented Newcastle side 2-0. Before the game, Keegan temporarily came out of the gloom that had descended upon him since the Championship had been given to Manchester United. 'I am glad the season is back. There's nothing like it and I never thought I would say that again.' As a statement of future positive intent it was more revealing for what it showed of Keegan's recent negativity. As it was Keegan struggled to talk up Newcastle's chances, what he lacked in conviction he attempted to make up for by pinning all on Alan Shearer's potential effect on the side.

'Everyone talks about the goals Alan scores but he is a team player. He enjoys his league football and his record is second to none. I am excited about him and Les. Alan doesn't set targets but hopefully he will score enough to win us something.'

There was a poverty of ambition about the words; Newcastle were now reduced to relying on one man for winning the Championship. It hadn't worked when that one man was Kevin Keegan; would it work now that the one was going to be Alan

Shearer?

Everton took full advantage of Keegan's defence. Watson, Howey, Albert and Beresford were the victims of an Evertonian assault and battery led by the giant Scot Duncan Ferguson, but it was not just the lamented lack of security at the back that let Keegan down. In every contest on the pitch Everton were coming out as victors. Shearer and Ferdinand were wrapped by the Everton defence whilst Robert Lee and even David Batty were defeated by superior grit in the middle.

Keegan, for so long the buyer of quality, was now paying the price of having too much. Never able to stick to Shankly's method of persevering with one set side, he was confronted by an excess of possibilities. 'There are other players and combinations I want to try but every time I put a team out I want that one to succeed,' he said.

The most unexpected victim of Keegan's search for the right formation was Peter Beardsley. Keegan's trusty 'Pedro' found himself watching games from the dug-out. Unable to sit down throughout a game he stood, strained and peered at the game. He may have been physically out of the game but psychologically he was as involved as any of the 11 first-team choices. If Beardsley was hurt or baffled by his exclusion he never let it show; of all the players who had offered Keegan their loyalty, Beardsley's was almost unconditional.

The start to the previous season had been wonderful, and many had expected more of the same in 1996/97, so when Wimbledon were beaten at home in the next match the presumption was that Newcastle were back on track. This was to prove a mistaken presumption. The season stuttered before it could start, by September 5 and the away game against Sunderland the press were indulging in their favourite activity again, writing off Newcastle United. According to the sports writers the team were looking at losing for the third time in four games.

But on the eve of the visit to Roker Park Keegan was back to his eloquent and involved self in considering what had been going wrong with his team. 'Maybe it's because of the type of player I was, but I like to see my teams going out to battle and scrap when they have to. I've told the players that if they keep playing the way they are then there won't be 5,000 fans watching them train. They will be able to get straight in their cars and drive home. There'll be no one there queuing for autographs. But I don't want that, I want the pressure to stay on them. I want them to stay in the limelight. I wouldn't swap my players for any others, and that includes Manchester United...although I wish I could start the season again.

'We want to be the big club that the supporters deserve. We could only be 90 minutes away from finding absolute perfection or then it might take 180. It may take even longer and then people can go on having a field day. At the moment most of the criticism has been fair. But we will make the critics eat their words. The general feeling in football is that we will get it right. I want this club to get back in line again as soon as possible. But you have to have force in this country. You have to be able to battle your way through on the bad days, the ties when it comes to the crunch. And in two games this season we have not done that very well. You can have all the ability in the world, but if you don't battle and work hard then you'll come out second best. I'm still looking for the right pattern. I'm still tinkering with a tremendous armoury. But the downside of having so many good players is that everyone has their own idea of what the team should be. We've been in much worse situations than this. But the expectation we have built at this club is huge now. We have not lived up to that this season, but we will.'

Keegan was canny enough to reassert his own combative credentials; the 'type of player I was' meant the small man who had fought on despite his size and social position, the Doncaster weakling who had become great, the poor man who had found wealth. Although David Batty needed no instruction in 'going out to battle and scrap' others were less inclined to fight to the finish. David Ginola certainly hadn't come up through the wet, cold and brutal world of South Yorkshire amateur football but Keegan had, and he expected his players to show similar toughness now that it mattered. And against Sunderland it mattered more than most. After implicitly criticizing the commitment of his players he then offered them his loyalty. But, as ever, the touchstone for Keegan was the support of the Tyneside public, who were placed above all else. Everything must be fought for so that Newcastle could become the club that the supporters deserved.

The rivalry between Wearside and Tyneside is felt with intensity, there is little humour about it. Sunderland fans take great pleasure in any set back for Newcastle United, and Newcastle fans would be happy to see Sunderland in the Northern League. So great is the likelihood of trouble when the two sides meet that for some time now the Northumbria Police have banned away supporters from Tyne-Wear derby matches. Such a deep divide is bound to transmute itself on to the players and the matches are usually more akin to Cup ties than league games.

The game was, as the pundits would have it, one Newcastle had to win. The list of what was at stake was formidable, regional pride, Keegan's reputation, the Premiership campaign and by now the team places of many of the Newcastle side. Given these circumstance it was no surprise that Newcastle's start was tentative and after 21 minutes Sunderland went 1-0 up through a penalty, and quite possibly could have scored three more as they outplayed Newcastle in the first half. Keegan is renowned for the effectiveness of his half-time pep talks, and this became another occasion when he sent out the same players, but in different formation, for the second half. Crucially Peter Beardsley was making his first Premiership start of the season and it was Keegan's little diamond who scored Newcastle's equaliser and David Ginola, so often questioned, from whose corner Les Ferdinand scored the winner.

Single victories may only bring three points but the psychological effect can be worth much more. Keegan was both angry and emphatic after the game, 'Our season started here. We had to scrap against it and we didn't even have a friend in the ground, just our bench. It was a character-building performance.' It was also a performance that ushered in a string of seven games without defeat which, added to the side's progress in the UEFA Cup, suggested that this time surely Keegan and his team knew what it took to succeed. Although there were blips, one match in particular was to suggest they possessed the right stuff.

No one apart, perhaps, from Kevin Keegan knew the home game against Manchester United was going to be Keegan's last battle with Alex Ferguson, but all expected it to be as intense an affair as usual with, if we were honest, Manchester United as the likely winners. How right and how wrong we were. Manchester United were slaughtered 5-0. They were beaten by such a margin that it's easy to forget that Ferguson's men did not play as badly as the scoreline suggests – when they were only 1-0 down they looked likely to equalise – it was just that Newcastle were ten times better.

Manchester United were dispatched in a game where Newcastle's defence were seldom given the opportunity to display just how ropey they could be. Shortly afterwards Keegan appointed the ex-Liverpool player Mark Lawrenson as defence coach. Lawrenson had made a living as, amongst other things, a television pundit, telling the nation just what was wrong with Keegan's defenders. The arrival of a coach for the defence seemed an unlikely admission from Keegan that he had been, if not wrong, then at least inattentive when it came to the team's defence all along. Keegan was well aware of the attention this would provoke, and when welcoming Lawrenson to the club he attempted to explain his motives. 'This club is so big now, that we would be burying our heads in the sand if we say we couldn't have defended better. Not just the last season but over the last four. But it's worked for us and our job, along with Terry McDermott and Chris McMenemy (who will stay on as first team coach), is to make sure that we get a little bit more...er... discipline at the back, but we don't want to lose too much going forward. Now, if we can find that then we've got a real recipe for success here.'

It was confusing stuff from Keegan. If, as he said, the system so far had worked for Newcastle then why change? His Hall-like excuse that the club was too big now not to appoint a defence coach didn't make much sense as the club had been big the season before. The answer was that last season's strategy hadn't worked, Newcastle had won nothing, if they had been the victors in half the matches that their defence had lost them they would have been champions at least once already, and either Keegan had come to believe that or the decision had been forced upon him. For Keegan finally to climb down from his so often stated insistence that there was only one way that the side would play football, and Newcastle and the world could have that or nothing from him, was a signal that most missed. When he signed Mark Lawrenson he abdicated some of his responsibility and with a man so committed to his own vision it was surely a precursor of complete withdrawal. Keegan was putting in place a provisional government to run things when he, the King of Tyneside, stepped down from his throne.

When you look into Kevin Keegan's face it contrives to be old and young at the same time, it is lined from five seasons of management, the hair that frames it is turning grey, yet the face remains boyish. It only appears to be as old as it should be when Keegan lets down his guard; he refuels himself with optimisms and enthusiasms that are stored up to guard against reality, which so far has been of coming second, of being beaten.

Just after the defeat of Manchester United Keegan was

involved in a promotional film for Adidas. By now he was the consummate media professional – he had been involved in the business for over 20 years. Uncomplaining he spent an hour in make-up as the girl changed him from a rather drawn man in his mid-forties into an old-age pensioner. It was a Monday morning and Keegan was a busy man, but he entered into the occasion with good grace and humour. He joked with the film crew and took the rise out of 'Pedro' (Peter Beardsley), did his filming in the minimum of takes, then sat down and immediately switched into an agonized existential mode that bore no relation to the man who had just been larking around. The make-up made him look older than he was, but it appeared to be an adequate reflection of the aged Keegan inside: 'I don't need this make-up to feel like I'm living in the year 2010.'

Newcastle had just beaten Manchester United 5-0. It was a time for basking in glory, but Keegan was weighed down by other concerns. 'In our game good results paper over a lot of cracks, you're in a better mood for everything. It takes me about a day to get over a bad defeat. The next morning I get up and I've got my family and private life, which is completely different from the football life. I soon get over it. I don't mind sometimes getting beat, when we've played well and been unlucky but have shown the club in a good light. But when you really haven't done that, then it's a long journey back to Newcastle. That's the way it should be, you shouldn't get pleasure out of getting beat, but you've also got to be realistic, know that you can't win every game.'

It was indicative of his frame of mind that Keegan should pick the morning after a great victory to consider the implications of defeat. There was a change in attitude as well from the season before. After the defeat by Liverpool at Anfield Keegan had talked of moral victory, of loving the way his team had played, now in a season when he had to win the Championship, he said instead, 'You shouldn't get pleasure out of being hard to beat.'

As Keegan sat wearily below the stadium, the rest of Tyneside was greeting Monday morning with talk of the Championship; if Newcastle could beat Manchester United 5-0 then they could do anything. Yet again Keegan was caught in the web of other people's expectations and yet again he tried to justify them. 'There's nothing wrong with it. Optimism is what it's called, and the Geordies are an optimistic race. You win a game and you want to win every game, you score a goal and you want to score five goals. I'm optimistic myself. Before we play Manchester United I think. "What's it going to be tomorrow? 4-0, 5-0?" Today we're laughing because we've beaten them 5-0. But sometimes you get annoyed with the supporters for thinking it can be that easy. You don't let them know that though. It's better to say to them, "The three points will do, just one more goal than them will do." Try and educate them just how difficult it is to go out and win 5-0. You know it's not an act out there, it's not a film, it's not stage-managed. It's real life, 11 against 11, competing against each other. We're trying to win. It's not like a pop group who go on stage and all the people there are their fans and like their music and that's why they're there. We've got to come out and set our standards every time we play, especially at home where the expectancy is that we should beat most teams.'

There are not many managers who feel obliged to temper their supporters' expectations, whether Keegan needed to do it to protect his own sanity or just to prevent more mawkish scenes of disappointed Geordies crying on Sky TV remains unresolved. Probably it was both self-defence and his obvious regard for the Geordies that motivated him simultaneously. Either way it was ironic that he should regret their expectancy of cavalier football and large wins because these were exactly the things that Keegan had brought to St James' Park. It was Keegan who created the creature that was now troubling him so, he was being hunted by his own offspring and if that caused him to zigzag from joy to despair he was willing tacitly to admit it. 'The financial rewards in football are greater, but the pressure is greater and the expectations are greater. Football's having a boom time, everyone's talking about it. But you can't say, "I want a private life, I want to be away from it." You can't have your cake and eat it. That's the way it is and we accept that. Every day I wake up looking forward to the day. Some people think I would be right in thinking I had the best job in the world. Other people say, "I wouldn't have your job for toffee." Somewhere in the middle of that is a realistic survey of what a manager's job is. The highs and lows, the responsibilities, the glory, the stick – they're all part of it. But I enjoy it. There are days when I think there are better jobs around and there are days when I think it's the greatest thing you could do. The mood swings are unbelievable at times, but you try not to show it.'

But of course Keegan did show it and as long as he did he was OK, it was only once he started bottling it up that he made the burden on himself intolerable. As if he was not under enough pressure already, he was adding more of his own. What he didn't bottle he attempted to deny. When asked the direct question that we all want to ask, what is it like to be a messiah? His face went down as he considered it. 'That's not something I take seriously. I don't think about the messiah stuff too much. What I think they're trying to say is that they've enjoyed the past five years since we've been here. It's been totally different to anything they can remember. That's the way I look at it. I don't look on this as anything other than a job which I think we're doing to the best of our ability.'

Between beating Manchester United and the Christmas fixtures Newcastle comprehensively beat Ferencvaros in the UEFA Cup, yet failed to beat West Ham at home and displayed all that was most alarming about their game in the 4-3 victory over Aston Villa. Nonetheless, as Newcastle went into the holiday period there was much for Keegan to be confident about, so his demeanour after a 1-1 draw at home against Liverpool was surprising.

Keegan slouched into the media reception room underneath the Milburn Stand. A cup of tea in one hand, the other in his pocket. The game had been nondescript, both sides had sparkled occasionally and both seemed happy with the shared points. If anything Keegan seemed slightly disinterested afterwards. Whenever Keegan came into a post-match press conference at Newcastle there would be a pause before anyone asked him a question, he had to chivvy the reporters into starting, no one wanting to be the first to open his mouth in front of the great man. This occasion was no different. Keegan uttered a few banalities about the game and then spent the rest of the conference presenting the tea lady with the traditional whip-round money. He drank more tea, then he was gone. As had his enthusiasm, without which he was lost.

In retrospect it was clear from his demeanour then that he would soon make his final, irrevocable decision to leave the club. Yet it would take something more dramatic than merely drawing at home to Liverpool to push Keegan past the limits of his own doubt. Keegan reacts well to defeat, as he has said, it takes him a day to get over losing a match, and if that match was lost by a Newcastle United side playing good football then he had little trouble accepting that on that occasion things had just gone against him. For Keegan it would not be drawing 1-1 that would prove unbearable, but winning by six clear goals. After a 7-1 victory over Tottenham he went straight to Spurs manager Gerry Francis to console him, visibly more concerned with his friend than he was with his team. Although Keegan was under pressure to sign a two-year contract or leave the club it was, he claimed, this moment that persuaded him to leave Newcastle.

As a manager Keegan always struggled most with himself in moments of victory; when he was saluted for engineering match wins out of delightful football, the time when one would expect him to crow, or at least allow himself the indulgence of a little hubris, was in fact just when he was most likely to crack. Victory for Keegan was always Pyrrhic and as he had approached Christmas 1996 he increasingly felt that the emotional cost of winning a football game was not worth it. Although Bill Shankly didn't believe his famous aphorism about football and life, like most of his utterances had said it for effect, it still signified a self-confidence in what he did and what he was that Keegan never came close to matching. Keegan never contrived to give his all to the game in the way that Shankly did. Further to that he always believed Shankly's dictum to be untrue. When confronted with what is, and whisper it softly on Tyneside, 'only a game', Keegan could no longer balance the equation between what a manager tries to achieve and any real sense of wider fulfilment. He finally left Newcastle after an uninspiring draw at Charlton, a more downbeat end to a dream is hard to imagine.

No one was shocked that the country had to wait for a tabloid 'exclusive' for Keegan's confirmation that the Spurs game was the moment when he finally lost the ability to accept the correlation between what he did and what it cost emotionally. That's Keegan. He may struggle with his inner balance-book but he has never had a problem with the real kind. His confessions read like clumsily ghost-written lines and were not a little tawdry. What's more, considering that Newcastle supporters have been living on a diet of rumour since he left, after all his lip-service to how great they were, he surely should have let them know, if not what had happened, at least what he felt about it. Still, what he did say makes instructive reading.

'Some people will be surprised, to say the least, to learn from me this morning of the moment Kevin Keegan decided to end his wonderful adventure with Newcastle United. Because contrary to widespread opinion, it was not triggered by the depression that comes with defeat. It struck me in the aftermath of victory. A thumping, famous victory at that. The day I decided I had to get out of football management was December 28, just after last

Christmas as St James' Park erupted in celebration of our 7-1 win over Spurs. It was the expression on the face of Gerry Francis, a man I like and respect a great deal. The elation of winning suddenly meant nothing when I looked at him and thought, "Oh no, how must he be feeling deep inside?" This was the man I succeeded as captain of the England team. A terrific manager who didn't deserve what he had to contend with that afternoon.'

That Keegan can miss the point so wildly perhaps proves that he was never really suited to football management. Who else but the manager of the team deserves to be blamed when his side loses 7-1?

'I wanted to go up and give him a cuddle...I didn't even attend the after-match press conference. I went straight home. And I knew that was it...that when you feel like that, you have to get out. I must stress that this was not the sole reason for my quitting Newcastle. I didn't go just because we scored seven and the effect it had on Gerry. But what the day did confirm was the feeling that had been growing within me for some time. I discovered in five years with Newcastle that the elation of winning is never as great as the disappointment of losing. For instance, when we beat Manchester United 5-0 last October it didn't replace the awful memory of losing to them in the Charity Shield at Wembley. So, despite all the speculation and various versions of events leading to the resignation that apparently shocked football, I want everyone to know the time and date when I realised I had to go,' he said.

Keegan, even when he is being ghost-written, can be charmingly disingenuous. There was nothing 'apparent' about any shock his resignation caused as it was blatantly obvious that it shocked not just football but most of Britain. But Keegan was still trying to talk himself down, reluctant as ever to admit what to the rest of us was inexcusable. He was a messiah. And when messiah's bunk off people are inclined to be surprised.

Keegan continued, 'And let me quickly impress upon Newcastle's incomparable supporters [and this is a phrase that really doesn't wash, as anyone who has heard Keegan talk at first hand about the Newcastle fans knows full well that such a stilted construction of other people's words as 'Newcastle's incomparable supporters' would not come with ease from Keegan's mouth], as well as everyone else in and around the game, that I believe my departure has paved the way for the man who can take the team that vital step further.'

Vital step further. If three words can sum up exactly what Keegan failed to do as manager of Newcastle then it is those three. In backing Dalglish Keegan also took the opportunity to suggest what he felt had been the undoing of his own ambitions. 'He [Dalglish] will need luck and all the other things that help a team become triumphant; the thickness of a post, a referee's decision here and there...Newcastle supporters have been so lucky to get someone who can help them achieve their dreams of winning a title or a cup. Those dreams meant a great deal to me, too, but I wasn't able to fulfil them. Those supporters don't need me to go into print with my appreciation because they felt about me just the way I still feel about them. As for me, well, I honestly felt I had taken the Newcastle as far as I could and the decision to leave was mine. Was I shoved? I don't want to go into detail about my resignation but no one has ever pushed me anywhere I didn't want to go. People will read into that what they wish. There will be a million and more interpretations and I can do nothing about that. But allow me to make one thing absolutely clear here and now. I have no bitterness towards anyone or anything at St James'...I am saying there is a time to come and a time to go. I have always believed a man must know when to get in and when to get out. The consequences of that hefty victory over Tottenham finally made up my mind that my time had come. The final parting came after two more matches, a three-goal win over Leeds and the FA Cup draw with Charlton. I took off the blinkers.'

Almost five years to the day after Keegan joined Newcastle, the crowds gathered again. The rebuilt stadium had changed beyond recognition, as had the club and the mood of the crowd. Mute incomprehension had replaced joy. The only sacrificial lambs on this occasion were the hopes of the supporters. The pre-recorded club-call message had just announced Keegan was leaving New-castle. It was the end of a footballing journey so intense and so unlikely that it had not only caught the imagination of Tyneside but riveted the whole country, and for the first time the man of the people, as if he didn't quite believe what was happening himself, wasn't delivering the news to the people personally.

On the way to that absent moment Keegan had come through a playing career that was a triumph of will over skill. Nurtured by the great Bill Shankly, Keegan went on to be twice voted European Footballer of the Year and set himself standards of personal achievement that would prove almost impossible to follow. He finished that playing career with two seasons at Newcastle United. As well bringing success he entranced the fans and started an almost claustrophobic relationship that, if truth be told, was one from which he would never be truly free.

After an eight-year period of unconvincing retirement that relationship drew him back to be adored once more. He saved Newcastle from relegation, gained promotion to the Premiership and ultimately created a team with as much international talent as any other in Europe. A potential giant. Yet as a manager he never won a major trophy and his unique and passionate involvement in what he was doing gathered as much attention as the wonderful football his side were playing. He proved either unable or unwilling to develop a lasting youth policy; he actually withdrew Newcastle's reserve side from their league, leaving no way for those players not in the first team to get match practice, and allowed talented youngsters like Darren Huckerby to escape St James' Park.

Eventually Keegan escaped himself. There is much speculation as to why he left Newcastle; the necessities of Newcastle United, the listed stock exchange leisure company, are commonly believed to have overcome the interests of Newcastle United the football club. That Keegan was forced out before the share issue because he would not commit to a further two-year contract is the current explanation for his departure among the speculators, although his own rather prosaic reasoning that he had enough and could go no further is perhaps the best excuse.

'You can't believe anything I say'

It took until 1970/71 season for Kevin Keegan to get a regular place in the Scunthorpe United first team. On his way to a professional football career he worked as a porter in a hospital and did shifts at the steel works. But once that career was underway from Scunthorpe to Newcastle, via Liverpool, Hamburg, Southampton and England, Keegan always made sure that he took advantage of every avenue that football opened to him. He was never beholden to the game itself, just the people that followed it and in particular the people of the north-east who invested so much of their own emotional capital in him and his football team.

Months after he resigned from Newcastle, Kevin Keegan spends his public time on the PR circuit and watching horses. He has put on a little weight, the infamous gooner is once more sneaking its way down his spine and he smiles, he smiles a lot.

Keegan is now free to view the stresses of management with some equanimity. 'I don't regret not being involved any more. I am very happy with my life, I had five good years and I'm enjoying my life now.'

When asked if he will be tempted to come back into management he replies, 'You're going down a road I don't want to go down now.' He also claims not to have watched Newcastle's run come to an end in the UEFA Cup.

'To be honest with you I didn't watch it, so you can't ask me about it. I was at a function. Please don't ask me to comment about it. I saw the goals afterwards but I didn't see the game, so it would be unfair for me to comment. It's somebody else's job to take it to the next stage, you know...that's the way I feel and that's the way it is. They've got Kenny Dalglish who is more than capable of doing that. You know his track record is brilliant. So I'm very supportive of him you know, I respect him, and I wish him all the luck in the world. Because you need luck...' At this point Keegan looks fleetingly embittered, and slowly he repeats the one fact that always defeated him, 'You need luck as well.'

Yet if Keegan had been denied luck, and a glance back to the 1995/96 season and the sheer amount of shots that hit the woodwork or were kept out by goalkeepers who seemed to keep the performance of their lives on hold for when their team met Newcastle would suggest so, how can he not bear to wait for his luck to turn? How can Keegan be personally contented with the succession of PR opportunities and stunts he's being lined up for instead of managing a football club? Keegan claims he is very content with his lot. 'Yep. I wouldn't have left if I wouldn't have been contented. I'm happy with my horse racing, I'd like you to see me in the winner's enclosure.' Hopefully the irony of that statement isn't lost on Newcastle United supporters.

Keegan talks about other managers very carefully these days. Glenn Hoddle is 'in a difficult situation', Kenny Dalglish is 'the best man for the job', and as for Alex Ferguson, 'Well, just look at his record'.

Keegan is a man who is deliberately paradoxical. He changes his mind from minute to minute, or rather he seems to, he likes to keep you guessing. An onlooker asks him if he will ever go back into football, 'Well, never say never,' he grins. Five minutes later when asked directly if he will go back into management he says, 'Nothing could tempt me.' When asked again he snaps. 'Right, I've had enough of this, I'm going home.' And leaves.

Several days later a report comes in of an interview he has given on South African television, 'I once said I would never go into management, so you can't believe anything I say.'

He'll be back.

Genesis 1:1–31 // John 1:1–18

FOCUS

'God saw all that he had made, and it was very good. And there was evening, and there was morning – the sixth day.' (Gen. 1:31)

The Bible begins with a fabulous announcement. Genesis is loaded with the biggest news ever. It tells us that we're not accidental, and that planet Earth is not a bauble spinning in space without reason. The words 'In the beginning God created' make up the most explosive sentence in history. And the Creator did not begin His work with a frown of disapproval: everything was declared *good*. In fact, the incredible, amazing, perfect God used Himself to model humanity on – we are made in His image.

And just as the Old Testament opens with news of God at the beginning of everything, so John opens his Gospel with words of God's ongoing care. God is both the Creator and the Rescuer of humanity.

Yet God's big story continues today. God continues to be active in His world – and now, as a follower of Jesus, you have a part in that unfolding story. The picture of

The Bible begins with fabulous news

Adam and Eve walking around the Garden with God is a good snapshot of what Christianity is. The Bible talks about us 'living by the Spirit', which literally means 'walking around with God' (Gal. 5:16). Of course, we can't see or touch God right now, and recognising His voice is a learned art, but make no mistake – you are not alone. And you never will be again.

PRAYER: Thank You, Lord, for this new life – not just of truths and ideas, but a life of walking with You. Lead me today, and always. Amen.

FREEDOM AND CHOICES

Genesis 3:1–24 // Romans 3:22–26

FOCUS

'So the LORD God banished him from the Garden of Eden to work the ground from which he had been taken.' (Gen. 3:23)

I have officiated at quite a few weddings, and it's always a moment of slight apprehension when both bride and groom are invited to speak up for themselves. 'Will you take this man …?' 'Will you take this woman …?' Momentary tension crackles. Will they go through with it?

No marriage can begin without the vital words 'I will' being spoken. Love is a free choice, and only as each person 'wills' to be wedded to the other can their marriage begin.

In Eden, it all started so well. But God's creation wouldn't be complete if there were no opportunity for decisions. As with marriage, to love someone involves the freedom of choice. We are humans, not puppets or robots. And so God built free will into His creation. And the first humans chose disastrously.

Choices have consequences; and now sin is part of the human condition for us all. We're all sinners at heart, literally (Rom. 3:23). That's the bad news. But there's better news. Christ died for our sins – that includes yours – and now is alive. And, as a new follower of Jesus, you have freely chosen to accept His offer of grace. Whatever bad you've done, it's been forgiven. It is scandalous, but true. That is why the gospel is called the 'good news'. Be glad – you've made the best choice of your life.

PRAYER: Lord, I praise You because, whatever my history, I have a wonderful future with You – and that includes today. Amen.

DAY 3 **AT THE CROSS**

Matthew 27:45–28:10 // Romans 5:1–11

FOCUS

'But God demonstrates his own love for us in this: While we were still sinners, Christ died for us.' (Rom. 5:8)

It happened again today. Yet another email arrived telling me that I can receive £20 million. I pressed 'Delete' instead.

Once we reach adulthood, we become increasingly suspicious of free gifts or impossibly good deals, fearing a catch somewhere. But there *is* such a thing as a free *life*, if not a free *lunch*. Trapped in the consequences of living in a sinful cosmos, there was nothing we could do to save ourselves from sin. Just as sin cut Adam and Eve off from God in the Garden, so we find ourselves separated from God. Trying to be good enough to impress God is a little like trying to lift ourselves up by our own shoelaces. It just can't be done.

Enter the rescuing Jesus. He came not only to die on the cross, but also to live the ultimate good life, showing us that we can once again live in friendship with God.

He came not just to teach, but also to give us the power to become transformed people, as we 'walk around' with Him each day. As He died on the cross the thick curtain in the Temple was ripped in half, indicating that an 'Access all areas' pass to God is now available to all who want it. And then He was resurrected three days later.

We could do nothing. At the cross, Jesus did it all.

PRAYER: Father, I praise You for the work of Jesus. You have done everything for me to live and die in You. We will always be together. Amen.

Choices have consequences

THE KINGDOM CALL

Matthew 6:1–34 // Colossians 1:1–14

FOCUS

But seek first his kingdom and his righteousness, and all these things will be given to you as well.'
(Matt. 6:33)

I am not that close to the royal family. By that, I mean they don't know me at all. I met Prince Philip once (a life-changing experience – for him …!).

Humour aside, I live in the United *Kingdom*, a territory where the reign of Queen Elizabeth extends. But when I first heard this phrase 'the *kingdom of God'*, I was terribly confused. The 'kingdom' was the main message of Jesus – but just what is it? It is difficult to think about a kingdom without there being a piece of land associated with it.

When Jesus speaks of the kingdom, He is talking about the sphere of God's rule and influence. As Christians, we are now kingdom 'citizens'. As we seek, each day, to put God's rule first, every part of our lives is affected by our decision to follow Jesus Christ.

Now we have a new purpose and our ambition is to see His

Real repentance leads to changed thinking

kingdom – His rule – widen. Our aim is to push back the darkness of injustice and oppression, as more and more discover the true King of kings: Jesus. We want others to come into this kingdom and discover His loving rule. And, not only that, we discover He is not a distant monarch. As we walk with Him by faith, we get to know Him. This is the kingdom: this is our new priority.

PRAYER: May Your kingdom come, in my life, in the lives of those I love and in the world. Let me be an agent of Your kingdom. Amen.

A WHOLE NEW WAY OF THINKING

2 Corinthians 7:1–16 // Matthew 3:1–12

FOCUS
'Godly sorrow brings repentance that leads to salvation and leaves no regret, but worldly sorrow brings death.' (2 Cor. 7:10)

'Repent!' It's a word that conjures up an image of an odd-looking chap harassing pedestrians as they pass by. In his hand, he holds a sign printed in old-fashioned Gothic script: 'Repent, the end is nigh.' It all seems antiquated and strange.

That's a shame, because repentance is a key to better, healthier days. Repentance is not only about being sorry for sin or even changing our mind about our morals. It's a word that describes us embracing a whole new way of thinking about everything, as we take on board a kingdom value system as followers of Jesus. As we will see tomorrow, this new life really is new and means that we accept God's perspective on the way life should be lived.

And although it does involve being sorry for sin as well, it is more than offering an apology. 'Sorry' is a relatively easy word to say. But being sorry doesn't necessarily mean that we are going to change. We can be sorry for damage we have caused, or because we don't like the pangs of guilt we feel. It is possible to be sorry every day of our lives – and yet continue in the same destructive behaviour. This is what Paul would call 'worldly sorrow'. Real repentance leads to changed thinking and changed living.

PRAYER: Change my heart, change my mind, change my desires and motives, that my life and behaviour might be changed today, loving God. Amen.

DAY 6 ALL THINGS NEW

Revelation 21:1–5 // 2 Corinthians 5:17

FOCUS

'He who was seated on the throne said, "I am making everything new!" Then he said, "Write this down, for these words are trustworthy and true."' (Rev. 21:5)

In the celebrated and controversial film, *The Passion of the Christ*, a poignant scene (birthed in the screenwriter's imagination, but rooted in Revelation 21:5) unfolds when Jesus stumbles as He drags His cross along the Via Dolorosa. Mary, her heart shattered by the agony of a mother watching her child go to His execution, rushes to help Him to His feet and, as she does, she remembers a moment when He had a childhood scrape, and how she had tenderly nursed Him. His face bloodied, Jesus gasps just one sentence to her, a few words that reveal the reason for the agony they share: 'You see, Mother, I'm making all things new!' It's a truth that Paul celebrates: 'Therefore, if anyone is in Christ, he is a new creation; the old has gone, the new has come!' (2 Cor. 5:17).

The call of Jesus is not a call to a patched-up existence but a renewed life, a renewed mind and a renewed lifestyle. This is radical stuff. When the first disciples bumped into Jesus, they signed up for a lifelong revolution. They made many mistakes still, but were on a totally new pathway. And, over the next few days, as we think about the value of obedience, the Bible, prayer and worship, it's because we want to live in that new life He promises.

PRAYER: Thank You, Lord, that I now have hope, purpose, direction and new life in You. Continue to show me Your ways, in Jesus' name. Amen.

DAY 7 FOLLOW THE INSTRUCTIONS

John 2:1–11 // John 14:15–31

FOCUS

'His mother said to the servants, "Do whatever he tells you."' (John 2:5)

I am constantly lost. I rather hope that this confusion is not genetically transmitted. When our grandchild, Stanley, was born, he was breech (chaps, that's upside down). This meant that a Caesarian section was necessary. Perhaps he's inherited my sense of direction, or lack thereof. Embarking on the short

journey that is birth, there was only one exit out – and he missed it.

Being lost on a car journey is horrible. Desperate, eventually I resort to pulling over and asking for directions. But then I get bored easily and so, while a willing stranger attempts to direct me with explicit instructions, my eyes glaze over and I fight sleep. For some reason, I seem to think that I know better. And then I get lost again.

And that's surely what gets a lot of us into trouble. As a new Christian, you have responded to Jesus' invitation to be one of His followers. Put simply, that involves listening to what He says about how to do life, and then doing it. Our obedience to Him demonstrates our growing love for Him.

God's commands are not friendly advice that we can take or leave. Moses didn't come down from Mount Sinai with the Ten Suggestions – they were orders.

Whatever He says to you, do it. He really does know what's best for us.

PRAYER: Lord, help me to obey You in everything. Amen.

DAY 8 THE VALUE OF SCRIPTURE

Acts 17:11–12 // Hebrews 4:12–13

FOCUS
'Now the Bereans … received the message with great eagerness and examined the Scriptures every day to see if what Paul said was true.' (Acts 17:11)

Christians believe that the Bible contains God's message to planet Earth. It's vital that your new-found faith is established on the truths of Scripture.

But that takes some care. If we don't learn how to use the Bible properly, we could think that adulterers should be stoned, slaves should be obedient rather than liberated, and life is all vanity anyway. Great damage has been done in history because the Bible was misused. The Bible describes itself as a sharp sword – and blades require diligent handling.

As Paul travelled to Berea, he discovered 'noble' people, noble because they examined the Scriptures daily to see if what he said was *true*. They didn't just *read* the Scriptures. The Greek verb for 'examine' is used of judicial investigations. For them, this was not mere intellectual interest – their studying led to believing. God is not interested in us merely adding to our bank of information. He wants truth to change our lives.

As we come to Scripture, we wash our minds in truth, correct our skewed perspectives, and allow the sword' of the Scriptures to cut into our lives, confronting and cleansing us. Establish a daily habit of reading and reflecting upon Scripture. God has spoken to us through His Word. Let's listen.

PRAYER: Teach me Your ways, that I might be changed as I discover Your Word of truth, Lord. Amen.

say what's on your heart

DAY 9 PRAYER FOR BEGINNERS

Luke 11:1–13 // Romans 8:26–27

FOCUS
'... one of his disciples said to him, "Lord, teach us to pray ..."'
(Luke 11:1)

Prayer – communicating with God – is essential to building our relationship with Him, but knowing how to do this isn't obvious. Even the twelve disciples of Jesus, who had observed His prayer life first-hand and were therefore in the best position to know how to do it, needed some extra help – 'Lord, teach us to pray', one of them asked. So, if we're struggling to know where to begin, let's not be discouraged.

God is a loving Father who already knows our needs (rather

like a good parent) but wants us to share them with Him anyway. And so we are invited to go to Him in conversation, asking Him to help us: as author Dallas Willard says, 'Request is at the heart of prayer'. Don't worry about asking too much – God encourages us to ask of Him. And don't get uptight trying to use the 'right' words: the correct way to pray is to say what's on your heart.

As a new Christian I was delighted and excited to go to God with my needs, and those of others. I had a real anticipation about what God might do and saw some marvellous answers to prayer.

And listen up. God sometimes speaks, but when that happens, it's not usually through a loud voice from heaven, or writing in the sky ... More often it's a quiet whisper, deep inside ... or words that jump off the page ... or a friend answers the question you've barely framed in prayer ...

Prayer is conversation. And conversation is the vital heart of any relationship, including our friendship with God.

PRAYER: Lord, I want to grow closer to You. Teach me to share my life with You; help me to listen when You speak. Amen.

DAY 10 WORSHIP

Psalm 100 // Romans 12:1–2

FOCUS
'Enter his gates with thanksgiving and his courts with praise ...'
(Psa. 100:4)

'Thank you.' Just two words that mean so much but, when missing, leave such a sour taste of ingratitude. God has done so much for us – and continues in His faithfulness every day. Thanks (or thanksgiving) is certainly appropria – and that's one reason we worshi

Although worship is far more than singing (our whole lives are to be an offering of worship), finding a means of expressing our thanksgivi and worship to God when alone and joining others to praise God in prayer, song, liturgy, poetry and ar are vital. As we worship, we remin ourselves that God is our number one priority; we celebrate wonderfu truths about Him as we sing and praise. Worship enables us to focu on God and, as we do, we have the opportunity to bring our lives into realignment with His purposes Sharing bread and wine together reminds us once again of what rea matters: Christ has died; Christ is risen. Christ will come again.

Worship is a way in which we express our love for God. Just as in any relationship, sometimes we will feel like expressing that love – and at other times we won't. Don't worry about that – it's part of being human. Worship anyway, because it's right, and not just because it feels right.

God is worthy – that means He's worth worshipping, whatever the weather.

PRAYER: Lord, teach me to worship You in all things, with the whole of my life. Amen.

DAY 11 TOGETHER

Ephesians 4:1–16 //
1 Corinthians 12:12–27

FOCUS

'From him the whole body, joined and held together by every supporting ligament, grows and builds itself up in love, as each part does its work.' (Eph. 4:16)

The idea of being together as part of a community is very attractive. Television shows like *Cheers*, *Friends* and even *Coronation Street* all have this theme at heart; it's important to belong. But community is actually God's idea, and it's vital that we

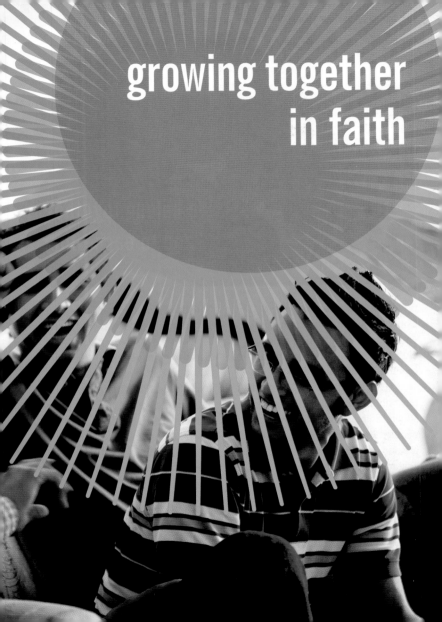

growing together in faith

We belong together, and to each other

understand the purpose of the Church, the Christian community, which is far more than a religious club where like-minded people get together to sing and learn.

God's purposes on the earth have not been fulfilled through superstar individuals, but through a people. Throughout history, as God created a nation – Israel – in the Old Testament (and then another 'holy nation' – the Church of Jesus – in the New Testament), we see that His plan has always been for a community of people to be a lighthouse in the darkness. They would be a living demonstration of what it means to live life with God in charge.

Christianity is not about 'flying solo' but rather 'formation flying'.

As we'll see (and you'll discover by experience), the Church is not perfect – nobody ever said it would be. The Church is an in-process, flawed, journeying people, just as we are. But being part of a church community is not an option for the Christian; it's the way God calls us to live – a family growing together in faith.

PRAYER: Lord, thank You for the family of God, the Church. Bless the church of which I am a part. Thank You that I am not alone. Amen.

DAY 12 BELONGING

Romans 12:1–5 // Acts 2:42–47

FOCUS

'... so in Christ we who are many form one body, and each member belongs to all the others.' (Rom. 12:5)

We live in a consumer society, where we expect to get things our way (my coffee can now be made **exactly** to my liking). Unfortunately, there's also a danger that we become church 'consumers' too: unless the music is precisely to our taste and the sermon the right length (and peppered with humour) then we'll complain (or maybe go hunting for a church that will exactly hit the spot). But with that attitude we miss the point. Just as being part of a family is not about everyone orbiting around *my* needs, so church is not a product to be picky about.

Obviously we need to choose a church with a style and approach with which we feel compatible, but let's remember that we need our differences and our variety to function well together. The image of a body is one frequently applied to the Church (also known as the Body of Christ). Why? Well, just as the parts of a body look different, act differently and each has a different role and function, so

do we. And that's the beauty of it. We all have our own unique contribution to make – from the smallest and youngest, to the oldest and (often!) wisest. So as you do what only you can do, everyone benefits. And that's what church should really be about.

So let's keep the consumerism for the cappuccino, and show commitment and loyalty to our church family. We belong together, and to each other.

PRAYER: Lord, thank You for allowing me to be part of Your family. Save me from selfishness; help me to want to serve, and not just to be served. Amen.

DAY 13 LOVE

John 13:1–17 // Philippians 2:1–11

FOCUS

'Now that I, your Lord and Teacher, have washed your feet, you also should wash one another's feet.' (John 13:14)

Jesus repeatedly tells us to love one another, for the church family is to be where the unloved and the unlovely find acceptance, respect, dignity and unconditional love. But what does that mean in practice? Perhaps an episode from the life of William Booth, the founder of the Salvation Army, can help us. Asked to pen a telegram to be sent to stir and exhort the troops in his army around the world, and mindful of the high cost of international communications, he was keen to be economical with his words. In the end, he wrote just one word: 'Others' – so summing up the serving, selfless attitude to which the followers of Jesus must aspire: to put others before themselves. Not easy.

But look again at the context of Jesus' words in John 13 – He had just washed the disciples' feet, clearly demonstrating His love and tenderness towards each one of them. When we realise how much God loves us and learn to receive His love, we are better equipped to love and serve others from the overflow of that love. To constantly give out to others from our own resources, not drawing on God's infilling love, can be a recipe for discouragement or burnout.

So remember, our Servant King who washes the filthy feet of His friends wants us, His followers, to be just like Him, carrying His love way beyond the boundaries of the Church to the poor and broken of the world. 'Others' is a word for our lives in the Church – and outside it too.

DAY 14 SPECTATORS

Ephesians 2:1–10 // Colossians 3:23–24

FOCUS

'For we are God's workmanship, created in Christ Jesus to do good works, which God prepared in advance for us to do.' (Eph. 2:10)

Yesterday I watched a panel of experts at a football match. They shouted when mistakes were made, and clapped and cheered when the solitary goal (for their team) was scored. They seemed to know exactly how the game should be played. There was just one problem: the only strenuous physical activity they engaged in during the match was collecting large slabs of pizza. They were experts. And spectators.

As you get involved in church life, you are not joining some multinational enterprise as a small anonymous cog in a very large impersonal machine. Nor are you

get your sleeves rolled up

there as a spectator – to watch everyone else perform. The Church is built on relationship and designed to be a family working together to see God's purposes fulfilled – and each family member has a unique role to play. We work and serve together out of love for God and for each other. Even though it is early days for you as a Christian, there are ways in which you can help. Don't just stand on the sidelines. It's harder work – but far more satisfying – to be involved rather than just observe. Volunteer to help out; don't be offended if you discover that there will be some tasks that those more mature in the faith have to handle. But do get your sleeves rolled up.

PRAYER: Save me from becoming a spectator, Lord. Show me the role You have created for me to play. May my efforts make a difference in Your Church, and in Your world. Amen.

DAY 15 MESSY CHURCH

1 Corinthians 1:1–3 //
1 Corinthians 11:17–22

FOCUS
'When you come together, it is not the Lord's Supper you eat, for as you eat, each of you goes ahead without waiting for anybody else. One remains hungry, another gets drunk.' (1 Cor. 11:21–22)

Imagine a church with this reputation: some people believe in weird, unbiblical doctrines. Others claim to know Jesus but show up drunk at the meetings. Few respect the authority of the leaders. And then it's so cliquey – instead of being one united church, it seems to be split into a dozen factions. It's hard for newcomers to feel welcome and to know where they fit. Doesn't sound too inviting, does it?

But that's exactly the way the church in Corinth was two thousand years ago. It was large, growing fast – and a total mess. As a new Christian, you'll have high expectations of church. And that's good because when church is working well, newcomers are being loved and accepted, and hospitality, kindness and generosity shown, it can be the most healing, transforming and supportive place to belong in the world.

But, unfortunately, nobody's perfect and church is not always like that. And high expectations can also set you up for huge disappointment. Remember that church will be messy because it's made up of people who might have no reason to socially interact – except that, in finding Jesus, they've found each other. And it is filled with in-the-process humans. Those who are part of the Church are not there because they think they've arrived – on the contrary, they have realised that they need God's rescue. The Church is not a gleaming trophy case, it is a field hospital in the middle of a battlefield. Don't be amazed when people fail. We're good at that.

PRAYER: Father, may Your Church reflect You – and may I do the same. Amen.

DAY 16 GROWTH

2 Peter 3:18 // Ephesians 4:14–16

FOCUS
'But grow in the grace and knowledge of our Lord and Saviour Jesus Christ. To him be glory both now and for ever! Amen.' (2 Pet. 3:18)

hospitality, kindness
and generosity ...

I am currently on a diet (I have been for a decade). I am tracking my progress on my phone, which monitors my progress against the specific target weight I've set. The pancakes and syrup this morning didn't help.

As we think for the next few days about growing as a Christian, one vital question is: What does a 'grown-up' Christian look like? If we are to aim for growth, we need to have a target – an idea of what we are aiming to become. Sometimes people talk about becoming more 'spiritual' as they grow in Christ, but that can give the impression that God wants us to leave our humanness behind. That kind of thinking means that we feel good about prayer, worship, Bible study and attending Christian gatherings, but believe a round of golf, a walk on the beach or a meal with friends is suspect. But the truth is that God wants us to grow into being healthily human. Humanity is His idea – He invented the human race! And the ultimate picture of what healthy humanity looks like is Jesus. God wants us to know Him, and become like Him.

And so characteristics like love, kindness, generosity, serving, faith: all of these are evidence of authentic growth happening in our lives. Knowing God, and loving more: these are the ultimate signs of maturity.

PRAYER: Lord, may today be a day of growing as a follower of Yours, as a friend to others, and as a healthy human being. Amen.

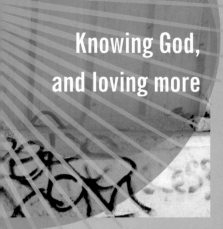

Knowing God, and loving more

Galatians 5:16–26 // Ephesians 5:15–18

FOCUS
'But the fruit of the Spirit is love, joy, peace, patience, kindness, goodness, faithfulness, gentleness and self-control.' (Gal. 5:22–23)

I am perhaps the world's worst gardener. I've never been able to produce anything much beyond a crop of prize-winning weeds. But even I know this much: I can plant seeds – yet I can't make them grow. Nature has to lend a helping hand and bring on the rain. Unfortunately nature only seems interested in the nettles in my back garden.

For the Christian, growth does not come about simply by our trying harder. The Christian life is not *just* about us doing the right kinds of things, but rather we need to be transformed each day into renewed people, who naturally do the right things because we are keeping in step with the Holy Spirit's activity in our lives. 'Just do better' is not the summary of Christian faith. 'Become better and changed by walking with God today' is the more biblical encouragement. Without the work of God's Spirit in our lives, nothing is achieved; nobody is transformed (John 15:5).

But, as we'll see tomorrow, that doesn't mean that we have no responsibility for the process of growth. As we learn to pray, reflect, be quiet, ponder and apply the Bible, we offer ourselves to the God who brings growth.

As we walk with God by faith through good and bad days, asking for His wisdom, trusting Him in storms, obedient and faithful – and getting up when we fall – so we grow. Ask God to fill you with His Holy Spirit today, and every day.

PRAYER: Fill me with Your Spirit, Lord; change me, mature me, empower me. Amen.

DAY 18 DISCIPLINE

1 Corinthians 9:24–27 //
Philippians 3:12–14

FOCUS

**'No, I beat my body and make it my
slave so that after I have preached
to others, I myself will not be
disqualified for the prize.'
(1 Cor. 9:27)**

Yesterday we saw that we can't just
change ourselves, we need God's
Spirit at work in us. But we do have
a part to play. As I write this now, I
am wrestling with my need to go to
the gym for an hour. Even though
I decided to run and lift weights
regularly some six years ago, I still
have to make what is often an irksome
choice to do it daily. I also want to
take some time to sit quietly and read
the Bible. As an activist, it's easier for
me to just dash on into my day.

Listening to Paul talking about
making his body 'his slave', it's clear
that growth only happens when
we take tough choices about the
way that we live. What our body
demands may be compelling, but
our bodies are not to be in charge of
us. We are to be in charge of them.

The world was captivated when
Michael Phelps took eight gold medals
during the Beijing Olympics. But he
achieved those dizzy heights by hard
work and making his body his slave.
In peak training phases, he swims at
least 80,000 metres a week, nearly
50 miles. That includes at least two
practices a day.

All that work was done for
a temporary reward. One day the
impressive row of medals will mean
nothing, whereas Paul reminds us
that we are in a race that affects
eternity. Being a disciple involves
being disciplined.

**PRAYER: Lord, help me to make
good, daily choices about my
life patterns and habits, and
so co-operate with Your work
in me. Amen.**

DAY 19 FREEDOM AND LEGALISM

Galatians 5:1–13 // Colossians 2:6–23

FOCUS

**'It is for freedom that Christ has set
us free. Stand firm, then, and do not
let yourselves be burdened again by
a yoke of slavery.' (Gal. 5:1)**

Talking about discipline means that
we have wandered into a vital but
dangerous subject. Whenever we
set goals for our lives, we can end

up creating lots of little laws, for ourselves and others. We start to believe, for example, that God will like us less if we don't pray for a certain amount of time. God might show us that a certain type of behaviour is not good for us personally (totally abstaining from alcohol is always going to be right for someone with a specific problem in that area), but before long we start to condemn others because they don't follow the same rules of life and faith that we do.

Some churches have been hijacked by this type of thinking. Lots of irrelevant regulations that go beyond what Scripture specifically asks of us are set in place and become the sign that we are really committed to Christ. This has always been a problem for the Church; how quickly we who have been freely set free by the shed blood of Christ meander back into following rules and regulations.

You are not saved and loved by God because you are always disciplined and pure; you are saved because of His great love and *what Jesus did for us all*. That love leads us to make disciplined choices – but our disciplines don't lead to God loving us more or less. Likewise, failure doesn't lessen God's love for you.

PRAYER: Lord, thank You for all that You have done. Save me from straying into thinking that I can somehow earn Your love by my own efforts. Amen.

Christ has set us free

THINKING ABOUT FAITH

Ephesians 4:17–32 // 1 Corinthians 14:20

FOCUS

'So I tell you this, and insist on it in the Lord, that you must no longer live as the Gentiles do, in the futility of their thinking.' (Eph. 4:17–18)

Meditation is a word that tends to conjure up images of an ethereal-looking person sitting, cross-legged, reflecting on the universe. But, as Christians, it's important that we learn to meditate – to think carefully – about God, about our lives and about what we believe. It's vital that we question, investigate and think about our faith, rather than accept a fill-in-the-blank Christianity that others spoon-feed us. Jesus constantly provoked questions; He didn't just make announcements of truth, but nudged those who were seeking truth to wrestle with challenging ideas.

Thinking Christianly is not just what Christians happen to think about things – because we can be wrong, as history has repeatedly proven. There was a time when 'Christian thinking' (the popular Christian consensus) was that slavery was acceptable. (We touched on that in Day 8.) William Wilberforce and others brought that outrageous notion into question. And then Christian thinking is never noncommittal; it is not vague; our thinking leads us to action.

Don't just accept that what others tell you about faith must be true. Ask God to help you to use the mind He has given you. Take time to reflect on your journey; consider starting a journal; and never be afraid to ask questions.

PRAYER: Lord, I want to submit my mind to You; teach me to be still, to reflect, to think. Amen.

GOD HAS CONFIDENCE IN YOU

John 15:1–17 // Matthew 4:18–22

FOCUS

'You did not choose me ... I chose ... and appointed you to go and bear fruit ... that will last. Then the Father will give you whatever you ask in my name.' (John 15:16)

It's a television show that has taken Britain by storm. *The Apprentice* sees a number of assorted hopefuls compete for an opportunity to work for multimillionaire Lord Alan Sugar.

we'll never, ever, be alone again

But the television show isn't really about apprenticeship at all. An apprentice is invited on a journey with a master, to watch what they do and emulate it. Lord Sugar doesn't go anywhere, except to the boardroom and to a few locations where he gives his instructions. But Lord Sugar does want to 'hire' team players, even if the process of finding them involves some bristling competitiveness. And he's relentless: mess up, and you may face the pointed finger and hear the ominous words: 'You're fired!'

Jesus was a rabbi with apprentices. Like the other rabbis of His day, He invited His disciples to join Him on a training scheme that wasn't contained in the cloisters or the traditional classroom. Quite unlike the rabbis of His day, Jesus did not wait for applicants to come to Him but He chose them – and they were not the cream of the crop but just ordinary working men.

But His choosing of them was a great sign of hope. A rabbi's call meant that he actually believed that the chosen one could fulfil the apprenticeship. Jesus believes in us. And He doesn't just send us out but comes with us, by His Spirit. That's good news for today. Whatever may come, Jesus wants us on His team and promises that we'll never, ever, be alone again.

PRAYER: Thank You, Lord, for 'taking me on' as Your apprentice. Teach me more about You today. Amen.

DAY 22 FAITH AND SUFFERING

2 Corinthians 6:1–13 // John 16:33

FOCUS

'Rather, as servants of God we commend ourselves in every way: in great endurance; in troubles, hardships and distresses.'
(2 Cor. 6:4)

There are some Christians who insist that if we have enough faith we can avoid suffering. After all, we, the champions of faith, are the King's kids and if our loving heavenly Father (who is rich beyond compare) really cares about us, and if we stick close to Him, then surely we'll enjoy the best and escape pain, won't we? The notion is that we can always expect to be rich and pain-free.

Wrong. Very wrong. Paul had plenty of faith. And yet look at the lists of the trials and tribulations he went through. Right away we see that he didn't escape or avoid them and he was honest about the reality of them. Apparently Paul was also battling 'we triumph while others suffer' teaching in Corinth (hence his use of the word 'triumphal' in 2 Corinthians 2:14). But he was unafraid to list the terrible experiences he'd had – in fact his times of suffering for the gospel are presented like authentic credentials. In what looks like weakness, he actually demonstrates true faith and trust. (Come to think of it, some of the greatest people of faith I've met have been confined to hospital beds.)

If you're suffering, don't let anyone tell you that you must be out of God's will or lacking in faith. Paul suffered. And he really was a champion.

PRAYER: In suffering as well as blessing, may I be found faithful, Lord. Amen.

DAY 23 TEMPTATION

Genesis 3:1–24 // 1 Corinthians 10:12–13

FOCUS

'The serpent was more crafty than any of the wild animals the LORD God had made. He said to the woman, "Did God really say, 'You must not eat from any tree'?"'
(Gen. 3:1)

If you have a pulse, you'll be tempted. What entices you may have no attraction for me – we're all different. But just as Paradise was blighted by temptation, so we will have to battle it in our everyday lives. There is a force of evil at work (in fact, we are living our lives in a spiritual battleground – see Ephesians 6:10–18) and the agenda is to drag us into the rebellion and madness of sin.

Notice the tactics of the tempter in this episode. First of all the serpent exaggerates the command of God, suggesting that He had said all the fruit in the garden was off-limits to the first couple. But that was a lie. Temptation can be strong when we feel overwhelmed; when we lose hope because we worry that what God asks of us is too much. That's why legalism (where rules that do not come from God are created) is so dangerous. When legalism overwhelms, people give up and, ironically, more sin results from their despair. And it's possible that exaggeration was also implied in Eve's statement, 'We must not eat of the fruit or even touch it' – but God did not say that either. It was only eating the fruit that was forbidden.

God wants us to be able to say 'No', not because He's a killjoy, but because He really does know what's best for us. When temptation comes, it comes with twisted promises and lies. Don't fall for it today.

PRAYER: Lord, help me, in the fight of faith, to know truth and see through the false promises of deception. Amen.

DAY 24 FAITH CAN BRING PRESSURE

Luke 5:27–32 // John 15:18–27

FOCUS
'… and Levi got up, left everything and followed him.' (Luke 5:28)

Sometimes I feel as though I need therapy before switching on the television news. The daily arrival of yet more apocalyptic headlines wearies me. But here's some encouragement: the Bible was written mostly to people who were battling with persecution, exile, economic turbulence and a myriad of other struggles. It's a vitally relevant message to people under pressure.

We've already seen that Christians are not exempt from pressure – and some of us are experiencing greater stress because we are followers of Christ. That was Matthew's (Levi's) experience. A well-heeled, fat-cat tax collector with a big income, he had endless resources; 'a large crowd' came to the meal he

Don't be surprised when doubts come

James 1:2–8 // John 20:24–31

FOCUS
'But when he asks, he must believe and not doubt, because he who doubts is like a wave of the sea, blown and tossed by the wind.'
(James 1:6)

provided to honour Jesus and Luke tells us that it was a 'great' banquet. But now Matthew walks away from security and luxury because he wants to be an apprentice of the Rabbi Jesus. And while the fishermen in Jesus' team occasionally went back to fishing, Matthew never returned to his dubious trade. For him, in a sense, Jesus ushered in a massive credit crunch.

Sometimes being a follower of Jesus doesn't relieve pressure but increases it. And if we're in any doubt about that, consider the thousands of persecuted Christians around the world who are suffering bravely because of their love for Christ.

PRAYER: Lord, when following You is costly and painful, help me to be faithful. Strengthen and bring hope to those who suffer for Your name. Amen.

Sometimes Christians use language that makes it sound as though God speaks to them directly daily, and they seem oblivious to any possibility of doubt. But doubts are actually very normal. We call each other 'believers' which means that faith is required to live the Christian life. There are times when our emotions are low, when difficult questions threaten to overwhelm us, or disappointment with other Christians can nag at our faith. Doubt can gnaw at us when we are asking God about something – and He appears to be silent. And when others seem to be walking through seasons of massive blessing, but the landscape of our lives feels barren, then doubt can loom once more. And doubt can send us spiralling down – as we wonder whether we are the only ones who have these troubling thoughts.

Don't be surprised when doubts come. And don't feel guilty because you experience them. Thomas had spent three whole years walking and talking with Jesus, but still struggled. Your feelings are not the barometer of your spirituality; they come and go. One day you will see Jesus face to face, and all possibility of doubt will be banished forever. In the meantime, if you doubt sometimes it doesn't make you a bad Christian – it just indicates that you aren't dead yet!

PRAYER: Increase my faith, Lord. When times of doubt come, strengthen me; help me to trust in You. Amen.

DAY 26 PURPOSE AND GUIDANCE

Romans 12:1–2 // Isaiah 6:1–8

FOCUS

'Do not conform any longer to the pattern of this world, but be transformed by the renewing of your mind. Then you will be able to test and approve what God's will is.' (Rom. 12:2)

The other day I watched a tightrope walker at work. The concentration on her face, with what looked like a hint of real fear in her eyes, made me glad that I didn't take the career path (or rope!) that she has taken.

I used to think that following Jesus was like walking a tightrope, and that finding out His will and purpose for my life was difficult and dangerous. What if I took a wrong turn? What if I made a huge mistake – would my life be useless and ruined?

A Christian is someone who wants to follow God's purposes for their life – but the best way to do that is to relax. Stop endlessly looking for God's guidance, and look for God Himself, as you think, pray, reflect and worship. Offer yourself willingly to God – our availability is the biggest key. God looked for a willing volunteer, and found him in Isaiah. Take advice from other trusted believers. Ask God not only to speak to you, but also to grow wisdom in you so that you will increasingly make wiser choices. Get to know Scripture. We make thousands of decisions where there is not a clear biblical answer to direct our choice – but there are many where God has already clearly revealed in His Word what He wants. An increasing sensitivity to what the Bible says will bring greater wisdom.

PRAYER: Lord, I offer my moments, my days, my life to You and to Your purposes. Guide me in the way that I should go. Amen.

DAY 27 GIFTED

1 Corinthians 12:12–31 // Romans 12:6–8

FOCUS

'If the whole body were an eye, where would the sense of hearing be? If the whole body were an ear, where would the sense of smell be?' (1 Cor. 12:17)

As you grow in faith, you will discover areas of interest and concern where you will feel that you want to get involved, to change the world. But when we start to develop a strong sense of calling, there's a danger afoot. 'Calling wars' can break out. Suddenly we start to wonder why everyone else in our church doesn't feel as strongly about those things we feel passionate about – and conflict results. Those who feel that prayer is especially vital get irritated with those who are really committed to social action. Why are the social action people not spending more time seeking God? But then the social action people can see the praying people as vague, impractical airheads who need to stop praying and get on with feeding the poor. And so it goes on. Suddenly, the wonderful gift of diversity has become the primary source of conflict.

Let's realise that we're all different by design and respect each other's callings. When others don't share the same passion as us, it's not necessarily because they don't care as they should, but because they are wired differently. And God has done the wiring! Like an orchestra with a huge number of differently shaped and tuned instruments, we can get the job done as we co-ordinate, work together, play our part in harmony under God's direction, and faithfully share our gifts.

PRAYER: Show me Your purposes for my life, Lord; and, when You do, may I be grateful for the concerns and callings You give to others. Amen.

DAY 28 GOD'S HEART FOR JUSTICE

1 Kings 21:1–29 // Amos 5:1–17

FOCUS

'Then the word of the LORD came to Elijah the Tishbite: "Go down to meet Ahab king of Israel … He is … in Naboth's vineyard … he has gone to take possession of it."' (1 Kings 21:17–19)

God loves His world. And He calls us to do the same, which

means that the plight of the poor matters. It's not just that charity is called for. God cries over the injustices that are created by greedy systems, corporations and governments. And caring for the environment is vital; we Christians believe that we don't own the planet. God made the world. It has only been lent to us. Justice in God's world, care for God's creation – these matter to God.

We can get overwhelmed by the sheer scale of the needs of our world, and even think that concern for the poor is more about politics and government than faith. But we are quite wrong if we try to escape the call to seeing our world changed. Nathan confronts King David about his treatment of poor Uriah (2 Sam. 12:9), and Elijah challenges King Ahab and Jezebel, his wife, over the way they snatch Naboth's vineyard away.

Jim Wallis describes a graphic illustration of just how much the Bible has to say about the poor – and what happens if we remove God's care for the poor from the Bible we teach in church:

A student took a Bible and cut out every reference to the poor with a pair of scissors. 'When the seminarian was finished that old Bible hung in threads. It wouldn't hold together, it fell apart in our hands. This is our Bible – full of holes.'

We can't do everything. But we can do something. And act we must.

PRAYER: Lord, Your Word is plain: holiness without care for the poor is not holiness. Show me my part, that my world might be better. Amen.

DAY 29 EVANGELISM

1 Peter 3:15–17 // 1 Corinthians 13:1–3
FOCUS
'Always be prepared to give an answer to everyone who asks you to give the reason for the hope that you have. But do this with gentleness and respect.'
(1 Pet. 3:15)

Now that you've become a Christian, it's natural that you'll want to share your faith with others. But that can seem a little awkward. Perhaps we've all felt uncomfortable as we've walked past that strange-looking man who shouts at people on the street corner. We don't want to turn into obnoxious 'Bible-bashers'.

We don't have to. Be natural

in the way you talk about Jesus; He's a huge part of your life now. Aim to share your journey rather than win an argument. It's unlikely that you've developed 'religious' language yet – but beware! Often the best way to share Christ is by explaining what has happened to you, as people ask questions. Don't feel that every conversation has to lead to a conversion. It's our job to live beautifully with God's help and leave the results to Him. Pushing someone to make a decision is both rude and potentially unhelpful. Jesus invited people to count the cost before they decided to take the plunge and follow Him. We can't 'convert' anyone – that's God's job.

If you're asked a question, and don't know the answer, say so. Listen to the views of others with respect. Invite others to come and see the church you're a part of. It can be helpful for them to see Christians worshipping, learning and doing life together.

PRAYER: Lord, may my life and my words speak well of You, that others might discover You through me and through Your people. Amen.

DAY 30 ONGOING CHANGE

Romans 12:1–2 // 2 Corinthians 3:17–18

FOCUS
'And we, who with unveiled faces all reflect the Lord's glory, are being transformed into his likeness with ever-increasing glory … from the Lord, who is the Spirit.' (2 Cor. 3:18)

It's a saying that sounds so true: 'You can't get a leopard to change his spots.' In other words, what we are is what we are. We are stuck with sameness. Popeye the sailorman lamented his condition when he wailed: 'I yam what I yam.' All of

which is desperate news, especially if we are addicted, fearful, destructive or angry. We can feel that our behaviour is inevitable and there is nothing to be done. But it's not true.

The Christian life is a life of gradual change, as we are transformed day by day by the work of God's Spirit in our lives. We increasingly take on the likeness – the character – of Jesus. We have to cooperate – and that means admitting we need help. Praying that God will change us is the first step.

It's a lifelong journey. Don't get discouraged when you fail – get up, accept God's forgiveness, and determine to keep following Him. If there are areas of your life where you feel stranded or stuck, or addictions that need to be broken, talk to another trusted Christian about them. As a Christian, you have not come to the conclusion that you're perfect – in fact it's the opposite – you've faced your need for Christ in your life.

Know this as you continue your journey: you can and will change, and for the better!

We follow Jesus. Not Popeye.

PRAYER: Lord, as I continue a lifelong journey with You, cause me to change and grow, to be more like Jesus. Amen.

you can and will change

Copyright © CWR 2011

Published 2011 by CWR, Waverley Abbey House, Waverley Lane,
Farnham, Surrey GU9 8EP, UK. Registered Charity No. 294387.
Registered Limited Company No. 1990308.

The right of Jeff Lucas to be identified as the author of
this work has been asserted by him in accordance with the
Copyright, Designs and Patents Act 1988, sections 77 and 78.

All rights reserved. No part of this publication may be
reproduced, stored in a retrieval system, or transmitted,
in any form or by any means, electronic, mechanical,
photocopying, recording or otherwise, without the prior
permission in writing of CWR.

For a list of our National Distributors visit
www.cwr.org.uk/distributors

Unless otherwise indicated, all Scripture references are from
the Holy Bible: New International Version (NIV), copyright
© 1973, 1978, 1984 by the International Bible Society.

Concept development, editing, design and production by CWR

Printed in the UK by Nuffield Press

ISBN: 978-1-85345-584-1